joseph m. champlin

slow down

five-minute meditations to de-stress your days

SORIN BOOKS ™   Notre Dame, Indiana

Imprimatur: Most Reverend Thomas J. Costello, D.D.
Vicar General, Diocese of Syracuse, New York
February 11, 2003, Our Lady of Lourdes

© 2004 by Ave Maria Press, Inc.

All rights reserved. No part of this book may be used or reproduced in any manner whatsoever except in the case of reprints in the context of reviews, without written permission from Ave Maria Press, Inc., P.O. Box 428, Notre Dame, IN 46556.

www.avemariapress.com

International Standard Book Number: 0-87793-604-8

Cover and text design by Brian C. Conley

Printed and bound in the United States of America.

Library of Congress Cataloging-in-Publication Data is available from the Library of Congress

Champlin, Joseph M.
  Slow down : five-minute meditations to de-stress your days / Joseph M.Champlin.
      p. cm.
  Includes index.
  ISBN 1-893732-78-9 (pbk.)
  1. Spiritual life--Catholic Church. 2. Meditation--Catholic Church.
I. Title.
BX2350.3 .C42 2003
242--dc22
                                                      2003021129

Introduction

A guarantee accompanies this small book.

Here is how that warranty works: Use the publication daily, or at least regularly, 101 times, setting aside five-minutes for prayerful reflection on each occasion. If at the end of these 101 sessions you do not experience a perceptible reduction in the symptoms of stress, then write the author at his address in the afterword and he will send you by return mail a check covering the cost of the book.

Basis for the Boast

This bold guarantee may seem like an author's fanciful boast or a publisher's marketing ploy. However, the offer rests upon a solid secular and spiritual basis.

Some years ago the leaders of the Transcendental Meditation movement asked Harvard Cardiologist Dr. Herbert Benson to conduct a study about the therapeutic effects of its practices. The research physician at the start felt skeptical about this idea, but they offered him a lucrative contract for the study so he agreed to undertake the project.

The results made him a believer. He discovered that people who practice meditation once or twice a day experience a measurable reduction in the extreme signs of stress, for example, blood pressure, heart beat, and sleep patterns.

From a purely secular or natural aspect, therefore, daily periods of prayerful reflection tend to reduce stress.

Those who strive to pause quietly for a significant period of time each day out of spiritual or supernatural motives likewise confirm the calming effects of that discipline.

Jesus often withdrew from his busy preaching and healing ministry to pray. After curing a leper of his disease and great crowds of their ailments, he withdrew to a deserted place for prayer. Before selecting the twelve apostles and continuing his public work, he went off to a mountain and "spent the night in communion with God." (Luke 5:12–16, 6:12–19).

When those twelve followers returned from teaching and healing missions, they excitedly spoke to Jesus of their great successes. His response, however, was: "Come away by yourselves to a deserted place and rest a while." And they did so. (Mark 6:30–32).

Close followers of Christ ever since have imitated his example and words.

St. Francis, after busily preaching and advising, regularly had recourse to an isolated spot in Assisi where he spent a lengthy time alone in prayer.

Protestant preacher and pastor David Wilkerson began praying late one night instead of watching a televised movie rerun and states that his life was never the same again.

The late Archbishop Fulton J. Sheen called those sixty uninterrupted minutes of prayer the hour that made his day.

Mother Teresa of Calcutta insisted that the members of her Missionaries of Charity fit their work among the poorest of the poor between substantive periods of quiet meditation at the beginning and end of each day.

Popular spiritual writer Father Henri Nouwen concluded that unless we have some time set aside for God and God alone each day, we will not be able to convert our unceasing thoughts to unceasing prayer or to transform our constant work into a constant awareness of God's presence in our lives.

These people found time for prayerful reflection each day because of spiritual or supernatural motivation. But all would concur that these quiet periods simultaneously center their hearts, calm their emotions, and still their souls.

A Radio Beginning

These spiritual suggestions began as sixty-second commercial radio spots, only later to appear in neighborhood newspapers and, now, be combined and adapted for this book.

Two years ago, a creative advertising executive suggested I do something on the radio and thus become a spiritual voice in the midst of our secular world.

In response to that idea, an account executive for a local station developed an agreement for three purchased spots at 5:43 P.M., a prime time slot (people driving home), on Monday, Wednesday, and Friday. These same messages would then be broadcast several dozen times that week as a public service at different occasions throughout the day and on an affiliated station.

Having made that arrangement, I next held an hour-long focus session with a dozen of the station's marketing and production personnel. We decided that the messages should not be merely psychological, but truly theological and spiritual, yet not denominational. They judged that stress was a main concern of listeners, but added about a hundred other potential topics. Listeners to this news and talk show station are generally older than thirty-five, and roughly half of them are men. A staff person developed the following tag line to conclude each message: "You may have tried everything else; why not try God?"

The response has been remarkably positive. Over the two years since we began the messages, barely a day goes by without an unsolicited word of praise about the spots. For example, our county executive wrote recently, "I especially enjoy listening to your spiritual moments for a stress-filled society." A bank teller could not remember the content, but said it gave her a lift. One seriously ill young man in a nursing home, who had never met me, recognized my voice as I entered his room and recited with excitement the commercial's tag line.

A year after we began, the publisher of several neighborhood newspapers praised the messages and expressed a desire to carry them in his weekly publications. Today the spot being aired that week also appears in those papers.

Several months ago, leadership people at Ave Maria Press learned of these spots, read a few samples, and concluded that with some editing and adaptation they could result in a small, but attractive book of helpful reflections.

The Psalms

The most major addition to these spiritual suggestions was the inclusion of a few words from the Psalms or even, in some instances, an entire psalm for each day's reflection.

The Psalms are not readings or prose prayers, but poems of praise designed essentially to be sung. Their purpose, therefore, is not simply to present ideas for the mind, but to move the heart as songs do. Even when we only read or recite rather than sing the verses, these words possess great power "to raise the mind to God, to inspire devotion, to evoke gratitude in times of favor, and to bring consolation and courage in times of trial"(General Introduction for the Liturgy of the Hours, article 100.)

All of the fundamental stirrings of the human heart have been captured by the psalms—longing and gratitude, praise and remorse, sadness and joy. Even if, however, on a given day, the psalm excerpt provided in this book does not reflect the reader's own current sentiment, memory of past occasions or pondering other people's situations should make the passage pertinent.

Using this Book

For the most effective use of this book, here are my recommendations:

1. Set aside five minutes of the day for reflection. If possible, the same five minutes each day.
2. Find a quiet space, where you probably will not be interrupted.
3. Get comfortable, but sit erect.
4. Take two deep breaths and exhale. Repeat.
5. Inhale a third time, and sense that you are inhaling God's goodness and light. Exhale evil and darkness.
6. Read the message. Perhaps, in some cases, read it a second time.
7. Move on to the spiritual suggestion and God's Word.

8. Spend the remaining moments reflecting upon the message and the suggestion.
9. Before finishing, reread the psalm verse.
10. Try, during the day, to recall occasionally a word or phrase from God's Word.

Father Joseph M. Champlin

Syracuse, New York

Christmas 2002

Day 1

Daily Prayer and Personal Peace

Leaders of the Transcendental Meditation movement asked Harvard Cardiologist Herbert Benson to conduct a study for them. The topic for his research was: Do those who practice this type of reflective prayer show any perceptible reduction in the signs of stress?

Benson felt skeptical about the project, but it was a lucrative contract so what could he lose?

His findings made Benson a believer. He discovered that those who meditate for a short period of time once or twice each day have a measurable reduction in the external symptoms of stress.

Mother Teresa of Calcutta is a good example: How could she be so serene in the midst of such stress? The answer: She daily spent a quiet hour with her God before and after working for the poorest of the poor.

A few minutes for prayer each day seems to reduce stress and bring peace.

Spiritual suggestion:

Set aside five quiet minutes today for reflective prayer.

God's Word:

Answer when I call, my saving God.
In my troubles, you cleared a way:
show me favor; hear my prayer.

PSALM 4:2

Stress and Serenity

Someone posed these questions to Mother Teresa of Calcutta: "Do you ever feel overwhelmed when you see so many little babies or deathly sick persons abandoned in the street? Are you sometimes stressed out by the countless demands poor people place upon you?"

This saintly, serene woman, whose focus was totally upon God and the poorest of the poor, responded: "No. You can only do what you can do." Her words might help, if we are driving home from a stress-filled day, or are in the kitchen rushing to prepare dinner for the family, or simply feel tense with so many things to do and seemingly not enough time in which to do them.

You can only do what you can do.

Spiritual suggestion:

At stress-filled moments today, remember the advice of the busy, but always serene, Mother Teresa of Calcutta: You can only do what you can do.

God's Word:

God is our refuge and our strength,
an ever-present help in distress.

PSALM 46:1

Gratitude

A single mother of three children recently hosted a party celebrating her daughter's ninth birthday. She worked hard to make this a wonderful event with special food, games, and prizes.

The cluster of boys and girls in her house seemed to have a great time. But at the end and afterwards the mother was crestfallen. Not a single youngster said, "Thank you." No parent called later with a word of appreciation. There were no notes of gratitude from adults or children. The saddened mother wondered why.

Have we ceased to be grateful? Have we failed to train our young people to say "thank you"?

A spirit of gratitude can make us realize that everything comes from God. It helps curb our self-centeredness. It warms the hearts of the gift givers.

Being grateful draws us closer to God, to ourselves, and to others.

Spiritual suggestion:

During today's prayer time, recall three recent gifts and thank God for them.

God's Word:

We thank you, God, we give thanks;
we call upon your name,
declare your wonderful deeds.

PSALM 75:2

Guilt and Forgiveness

Guilt is a painful burden. It penetrates the core of our being and stays with us. Fortunately, according to some of our major religious traditions, God is willing, almost anxious to forgive sin, remove guilt, and bring peace.

In the Jewish tradition, the Hebrew Scriptures or Old Testament, God is compassion, kindness, with a mercy that endures forever.

In the Christian tradition, the New Testament of the Bible, God comes to save us, to forgive us, to set us free.

In the Muslim tradition, a favorite title for the awesome, transcendent God is "The Merciful One."

While guilt from our bad choices is a very painful reality, a merciful God can forgive sins, dissolve guilt, and fill us with a joyful peace.

Spiritual suggestion:

Let go of any guilt over past sins, allowing a merciful God to forgive and heal you.

God's Word:

Have mercy on me, God, in your goodness;
in your abundant compassion blot out my offense.
Wash away all my guilt;
from my sin cleanse me.

PSALM 51:3–4

Self Esteem

Many of us struggle with a shaky self-esteem.

It shows in several ways.

We do not take compliments well.

We brood over one critical remark in a review and forget the nine positive comments made about us.

We find it hard to let someone love us.

How do we replace a weak self-image with a healthy self concept?

Recognizing that we are unique persons is a start.

Feel your fingertips. No one else in the whole world has your fingerprints.

Nor does anyone else have your DNA strands.

The Bible states that God calls us by name, holds us in the palm of his hand and tells us we are glorious, precious, and loved by the Creator.

Spiritual suggestion:

During your prayer today, feel your fingertips and reflect upon your uniqueness before God.

God's Word:

I praise you, so wonderfully you made me; wonderful are your works!

PSALM 139:14

Suffering Evil in the World

A California driver, filled with road rage, recklessly pulled out of the lane on a busy San Diego freeway. Unfortunately, the vehicle left the highway, careened across the median, struck an on-coming car, and caused a massive pile up.

The tragedy killed an older woman and left many injured. However, one person walked away unscathed—a young lady of thirty.

For several years she kept asking: Why was I spared? How could God let this happen?

She wandered from church to church seeking an answer.

This explanation finally quieted her heart.

God gave us freedom. We are free to choose the good or the bad, to make careful or careless decisions. The accident was not part of God's plan, but once it happened, God was there bringing good out of this disaster. For example, it led that young woman to faith.

Spiritual suggestion:

When experiencing evil or suffering in the world, recall how God respects human freedom, but brings something good out of the darkness.

God's Word:

The Lord is close to the brokenhearted,
saves those whose spirit is crushed.

PSALM 34:19

DAY 7

Loving Others

During the finale of the powerful musical *Les Miserables*, a chorus from above escorts the dying hero Jean Valjean to his heavenly home.

While doing so, they sing "Those who love another person will see the face of God."

There were many times when this remarkably strong, brave, and caring man showed his love for others.

He unselfishly raised the orphaned Cosette to adulthood.

He went out at night with his pockets full and returned with them empty, having secretly given coins to the poor.

He prayed to God on high that Cosette's beloved Marius would return safely from battle.

The Bible commands: Love God with your whole heart and your neighbor as yourself.

Jean Valjean kept these commands and at the end of his life heard angelic voices sing: "Those who love another person will see the face of God."

Spiritual suggestion:

Today, reach out with love toward someone.

God's Word:

Trust in the Lord and do good
that you may dwell in the land and live
secure.
Find your delight in the Lord
who will give you your heart's desire.

PSALM 37:3–4

Forgiveness of Others

In Minneapolis, Minnesota, Donald Ehrlichmann, forty-four, and his son Michael, nineteen, picked up three young hitchhikers who seemed to need help.

A few blocks later one hitchhiker pulled out a gun and demanded money. The father then deliberately swerved the car into a tree, jumped out, and ran shouting for help, leaving his son in the front seat dazed from the impact.

The hitchhiker fired three shots, killing the father.

At the subsequent funeral, Ehrlichmann's family asked friends and society to forgive the hitchhikers.

His widow also offered to take the three young men into her home, if this was the kind of love they could understand and needed.

Later, the grieving woman wrote an open letter addressed to the three boys who murdered her husband. She concluded: "Know that God forgives you and that my family and I forgive you—then go out and make something worthwhile out of the rest of your lives. God keep and bless you."

Spiritual suggestion:

Think of someone who has hurt you in the past, and with God's help forgive that person.

God's Word:

Lord, you are kind and forgiving,
most loving to all who call on you.
                              PSALM 86:5

The Power of Prayer

A nationally known leader has experienced the power of prayer.

In his mid-fifties, he starts each day on his knees praying.

He reads the Bible every morning and studies a daily lesson from scripture.

He prays frequently in his office at work.

He often asks an advisor to lead a prayer at meetings.

He sometimes prays over the phone with a friend who is a minister.

People close to him say that faith and prayer changed his life twenty years ago. Prayer helped him quit drinking, find his true vocation in life, and check his fiery temper.

In a very challenging position today, prayer keeps him humble, tolerant, and serene.

This person has experienced the power of prayer. His code name is POTUS, the current President of the United States, George W. Bush.

Spiritual suggestion:

Try reflecting upon the example of others to deepen your own confidence in the power of prayer.

God's Word:

I will call upon God,
and the LORD will save me.
At dusk, dawn, and noon
I will grieve and complain,
and my prayer will be heard.

PSALM 55:17–18

DAY 10

Violence in the City

I jog several times each week around our center city neighborhood. The three-mile run takes me, an older white man, through a mostly poor African-American community.

Over six years I have followed the identical route without any violence, except for one occasion.

On that day I had paused at a corner for the light to change and was chatting with three men in front of a grocery store. Suddenly, I felt a slight hit on my head and realized that a teenage boy had pulled off my ski cap and run across the street. He and his young companion stopped and stood a hundred feet away.

Immediately one of the men said to the thief: "Give the hat back to the man." There was no response. He repeated the command. Again no response.

Then the thief's friend crossed the street, took the cap, and slowly returned it to me.

I said "Thank you."

He replied, "You're welcome."

I resumed my run home seeing this as a God-filled rainbow moment, but unsure of what had really happened.

Spiritual suggestion:

Recall a surprising, positive experience, like a rainbow in the midst of some darkness, that was a sign of God's loving presence in your midst.

God's Word:

The heavens declare the glory of God;
the sky proclaims its builder's craft.

PSALM 19:2

Caring or Competitive

Our worldview leads us to be truly caring or excessively competitive.

The first view sees the world around us like a huge sky with an unlimited number of stars. Each star represents a person with many gifts.

When that person uses these gifts well, the star shines brightly. When that person uses those gifts poorly, the star does not shine at all.

My world is thus much more beautiful when the star shines and less beautiful when the star does not.

That makes me glad when another person succeeds and sad when another person fails. It can lead me to be truly caring.

The other view sees the world around us like a huge pie, but with only a limited number of slices, each slice representing a person with gifts. If you have a slice, I therefore have less; if you don't have a slice, I have more.

That can make me sad about your successes, happy about your failures. It can make me excessively competitive.

The ideal, of course, is to view our world as a huge sky with an unlimited number of stars rather than a mammoth pie with only a limited number of slices.

Spiritual suggestion:

Reflecting upon the sky or a pie, ask yourself:
Are you truly caring or excessively
competitive?

God's Word:

When I see your heavens, the work of your
fingers,
the moon and stars that you set in place—
What are humans that you are mindful of
them,
mere mortals that you care for them?

PSALM 8:3–5

The Love of Giving and Receiving

Love involves giving, but sometimes requires receiving.

Love basically means giving, being unselfish, thinking of another or others, instead of oneself.

Just before World War II, Tom Broderick could have obtained a medical student deferment.

He might have selected a less risky branch of the service.

He chose neither of those easier options.

As a result, he gave up, not his life, but his eyesight forever during a battle in Europe.

Later Tom gave hope to many soldiers blinded through battle in Vietnam by describing to them his own successful family and business life.

My brother knows that a giving love sometimes requires receiving.

A doctor recently said to him "Friend, you are legally blind through macular degeneration."

Now he no longer can drive, read a menu or cut his own nails.

In this, and in many other ways, he must allow his wife to do the giving.

Love for him often now means receiving, allowing others to give to him, to love him.

Spiritual suggestion:

There certainly will be opportunities during this day to practice love by giving, but there probably will also be occasions for you to love by receiving.

God's Word:

I thank you Lord, with all my heart,
I bow low toward your holy temple:
I praise your name for your fidelity and love.
For you have exalted overall your name and your promise.
When I cried out, you answered;
you strengthened my spirit.

PSALM 138:1–3

Forgiving Others

Father Lawrence Jenco arrived in Beirut, Lebanon to help the poor, assigned there as program director for Catholic Relief Services. He was roughly kidnapped shortly after his arrival by terrorists who mistook him for a United States government official.

For five hundred and sixty-two days, his captors kept him blindfolded, beat him severely, and confined him in cruel, cramped quarters. They totally disregarded Jenco's advanced age and poor health.

Just prior to his release, Sayeed, one of the guards who had often brutalized Jenco, asked the blind folded priest, "Abouna, (that is Arabic for 'dear father'), do you forgive me?"

Jenco, stunned by the request, reflected, then replied: "Sayeed, there were times I hated you. I was filled with anger and revenge for what you did to me and my brothers. But God said that I was not to hate, but to love you. I need to ask God's forgiveness and yours."

Spiritual suggestion:

We all have been hurt at times by others. Once again, identify someone who has wounded you and ask God to help you forgive that person.

God's Word:

Help us God our savior,
for the glory of your name.
Deliver us, pardon our sins
for your name's sake.

PSALM 79:9

Perfectionism

Four people were playing on a beautiful San Francisco golf course with a spectacular view of the Golden Gate Bridge.

Each of them made a pretty fine chip shot onto the green. But all of them felt quite annoyed about their bad locations and swore loudly in disgust at their poor performances.

These negative reactions surprised a nearby person who had observed the scene.

A golfer himself, he judged that their shots, while not perfect, were actually quite good.

Moreover, he thought how many positives they were ignoring on that afternoon.

They were missing the beauty of the course, the spectacular view, the very ability to walk and to swing a club, the companionship, even the freedom to be away from work for several hours of golf.

An obsession with being perfect sometimes can cause us to lose sight of countless blessings that surround us.

Spiritual suggestion:

Ask yourself: Do I often or at least occasionally miss my blessings because I am preoccupied with my burdens or shortcomings?

God's Word:

The Lord is my light and my salvation;
whom do I fear?
The Lord is my life's refuge;
of whom am I afraid?

PSALM 27:1

DAY 15

Praying for Others

The nuns at the cloistered convent on Court Street in Syracuse live quite differently from most of us.

They never go beyond the convent walls, except on very rare occasions.

They rise before dawn and retire early in the evening.

They spend hours silently reading religious books and reflecting upon spiritual matters.

They each work on assigned tasks to support the community.

They eat sparingly and recreate simply.

And, as their main task, they go to the chapel at least seven times daily to worship God and pray for others.

For some these may seem like wasted lives. But who can say how powerful are their prayers for others? And visitors know that their faces radiate great joy and their hearts lovingly reach out to all outside the convent walls.

Spiritual suggestion:

Today, pray specifically for a few persons close to you.

God's Word:

Lord, my God, I call out by day;
at night I cry aloud in your presence.
Let my prayer come before you;
incline your ear to my cry.

PSALM 88

DAY 16

A Poetic Marriage Promise

We offer engaged couples an option for the wedding
service. They can write their hopes and expectations
separately, then have me read them during the
church ceremony itself.

One groom, a factory worker, composed this
poem on his hopes and expectations for their marriage.

> I cannot promise you a life of sunshine,
> I cannot promise riches, wealth, or gold,
> I cannot promise you an easy pathway
> That leads away from change or growing old.
> But I can promise all my heart's devotion,
> A smile to chase away your tears of sorrow,
> A love that's ever true and ever growing,
> A hand to hold in yours through each tomorrow.
> Two loving arms to shelter and protect you,
> The knowledge that I need you more than ever,
> And all the happiness that love can give you
> As, hand in hand, we walk through life together.

The love of husband and wife can reflect and
thus remind all of God's love for us. God's perfect
self-giving love is also a model for spouses in their
own relationship.

Spiritual suggestion:

Recall an instance of self-giving love between a married couple in your family or among your acquaintances.

God's Word:

Praise the Lord, who is so good;
God's love endures forever;
Praise the God of heaven,
God's love endures forever.

PSALM 136 :1–2

DAY 17

Addictions

Over the years several friends, colleagues, and parishioners have been addicted to sex, alcohol, or food.

Their lives were out of control.

Fortunately, they overcame their denial, admitted they had a problem, and took steps to manage the addiction.

In the process they learned these truths:

It is not their fault that they have this addiction.

The addiction will never go away. They are recovering, not recovered addicts.

They are powerless by themselves to correct the situation.

By using the aids available and depending upon the help of a Higher Power beyond themselves, who most call God, they can manage the addiction and bring their lives under control.

Spiritual suggestion:

Ask yourself: Am I so addicted to anything that it has control over me and takes away my freedom? What should I do about this?

God's Word:

I love you, Lord, my strength,
Lord, my rock, my fortress, my deliverer,
My God, my rock of refuge,
my shield, my saving horn, my stronghold!

PSALM 18:2–3

Faith

Mesa Airlines sometimes flies a single engine Piper Cub from Albuquerque to Santa Fe, New Mexico. The pilot commented to the three passengers that the short afternoon flight should be a beautiful experience—a wonderful sunset, colorful rock formations, and a clear sky.

It was.

Imagine the three passengers:

The first doesn't even notice the magnificent sunset. His problem: So preoccupied with daily concerns, he has no time to smell the daisies.

The second observes: What a spectacular sight!

The third proclaims: Praise God from whom all blessings flow.

The same reality for all three. One went beyond and discovered the presence of God in the beauty of the world around us.

Faith does that. It goes beyond beauty and finds transcendence, experiences God.

Spiritual suggestion:

With faith, look beyond beautiful experiences and objects, recognizing God the Creator of all beauty.

God's Word:

Bless the Lord, my soul!
Lord, my God, you are great indeed!
You are clothed with majesty and glory,
robed in light as with a cloak.

PSALM 104:1–2

DAY 19

Being a Good Samaritan

Driving up South Warren street in Syracuse can be frustrating when the stoplights seem out of sync.

On one of these days I had parked, done some banking business, returned to my car, and was anxious to pull out into traffic and be on my way.

There were several vehicles waiting for the light to change, but when it turned green, none moved.

I grumbled at their slow responses and wondered why.

Then I saw the reason.

Someone was helping a developmentally disabled and badly crippled person across Warren Street in front of the first stopped car.

Here was a Good Samaritan helping someone in need.

Here was a Good Samaritan driver pausing patiently to let them pass.

Here was a grumpy priest forgetting for a moment the Good Samaritan lesson he often preaches.

Spiritual suggestion:

Good Samaritans help others, even at a cost
to themselves.

God's Word:

The law of the LORD is perfect,
refreshing the soul.
The decree of the LORD is trustworthy,
giving wisdom to the simple.
The precepts of the LORD are right,
rejoicing the heart.
The command of the LORD is clear,
enlightening the eye.

PSALM 19:8–9

A Best-Selling Prayer

An unlikely title topped the *New York Times* list of best-selling, how to, self-improvement, hardcover books for a long time. *The Prayer of Jabez* is that small, popular volume, with more than one million copies in print.

Jabez appears briefly in the Hebrew Scriptures or the Old Testament first book of Chronicles. In this short, two-verse encounter, we discover that he was more honorable than others and prayed earnestly for divine assistance.

So powerful and appropriate was his prayer that the Bible states: "God granted him what he requested."

In his remarkably successful book, Dr. Bruce Wilkinson describes in detail the short prayer of Jabez and how it can apply to every person's life.

Jabez asked God to bless him, expand his vision, support his work, and keep him from harm.

As we noted, God granted him what he requested.

Spiritual suggestion:

God responds to earnest, humble, and trusting prayer.

God's Word:

I trust in you, LORD;
I say, 'You are my God.'

PSALM 31:15

St. Ignatius of Loyola

Ignatius of Loyola was born the year before Columbus discovered America. During his early days as a soldier, he lived in a quite worldly way. However, wounded in battle, Ignatius experienced a conversion of heart while he was recovering.

He asked health caregivers for some novels to read. There were none available, only a life of Christ and a collection of stories about saints. Ignatius noted a difference when reflecting upon his past worldly life and reading these spiritual books.

The memories of older moments gave him intense pleasure, but after abandoning such thoughts out of weariness, he felt dry and depressed.

The books also gave him great satisfaction as he pondered imitating those heroic saints. But afterwards he felt, not dry and depressed, but great joy.

Ignatius then changed and began a very holy life, eventually forming the Society of Jesus or Jesuits. God became the center of his life.

Spiritual suggestion:

Ask yourself: Is God the center of my life?

God's Word:

As the deer longs for streams of water,
so my soul longs for you, O God.
My being thirsts for God, the living God.
When can I go and see the face of God?

PSALM 42:2–3

DAY 22

Our Awesome God

The Bible and the Koran tell us that God is mighty and awesome. Being near a lake or the ocean can give us an experience of that awesomeness.

Around 5:00 in the afternoon, a quiet calm seems to descend around any body of water. That can remind us of the deep peace and serenity God offers our hearts.

The beauty of a magnificent sunset reflected over the water arrests us, sort of stops us in our tracks. This, too, can lead us to the God responsible for such beauty.

The ocean, with its powerful surf, its waves endlessly rolling upon the shore, and its immense size can likewise raise minds and hearts to a mighty and awesome God.

Spiritual suggestion:

Reflect upon being next to a calm lake in the late afternoon, or watching a sunset over a body of water, or observing the powerful ocean, then praise a God so mighty and awesome.

God's Word:

O LORD, our Lord,
how awesome is your name through all the earth!
You have set your majesty above the heavens!

PSALM 8:2

Mortality and Courage

In 2003, cyclist Lance Armstrong was riding high on life. He won his fifth straight Tour de France, tied a world record, and made the front page of sports sections. After his victory in 2002, at President Bush's invitation he flew home to Texas on Air Force One.

But six years earlier, things were dark for him. A doctor told Lance, then twenty-five, that not only did he have advanced testicular cancer, but that it had spread to his lungs and his brain.

Such news forces us to face our mortality. We then also often make unreal promises to ourselves and to God. Armstrong told himself that he'd never curse again, drink another beer, or lose his temper. He was going to be the greatest, the most clean-living guy one could hope to meet.

I doubt if he has kept all these promises. But with great courage he underwent lengthy and difficult treatments. They worked.

That made his victories in France all the more significant.

Armstrong has now established a foundation to fight cancer.

Spiritual suggestion:

Think of someone experiencing an unexpected serious illness who was forced to face their own mortality and to find the courage needed for this challenge.

God's Word:

I believe I shall enjoy the LORD's goodness
in the land of the living.
Wait for the LORD, take courage;
be stouthearted, wait for the LORD!

PSALM 27:13–14

Addictions #2

Dr. Patrick Carnes published a book originally called *Understanding Sexual Addiction,* which had very few buyers. That is not a surprise. Even if the clerk put the text in a brown paper bag, most would still feel embarrassed purchasing the volume.

He changed the title to *Out of the Shadows* and it sold much better.

Any addictive sexual behavior, he maintains, follows a SAFE formula:

It is *secret*, creating shame within us.

It is *abusive*, hurting ourselves and others.

It is used to avoid or cause painful *feelings*.

It is *empty* of caring, committed relationships.

All addictive behavior tends to observe this SAFE pattern.

Recovering addicts believe that only a higher power we call God can free them from such a burden.

We may not be addicted to alcohol, drugs, or sex, but it seems that all of us have some addiction or attachment that limits our freedom. Even in those lesser, but still enslaving situations, we need the power of God to free us.

Spiritual suggestion:

Ask God to free you from your particular addiction or attachment.

God's Word:

Save me, God,
for the waters have reached my neck.
I have sunk into the mire of the deep,
where there is no foothold.
I have gone down to the watery depths;
the flood overwhelms me.

PSALM 69:2–3

Terrorist Attack

When we watched the World Trade Center's twin towers topple or heard personal stories of grief caused by the September 11, 2001 attack on America, the question "Why God?" almost automatically came to our lips. "Lord, how could you let this happen?"

We might imagine God responding: "I am weeping with you. This is not my doing. As I said to you in the Bible: 'My plans for you are peace and not disaster.'"

"But," the Lord would continue, "I give every person freedom—to choose good or evil. I will not take that freedom away."

"However, I am very close to you all, especially those in trouble. I give strength and guidance to the burdened. And out of this darkness, I bring light."

God could have concluded: "Have you noticed the heroic workers, the many volunteers, the thousands praying?"

Many or most troubles come from our own free, but bad choices, or the free, but bad choices of others. Yet God is always there, respecting our freedom, but bringing good out of the bad, light out of the darkness.

Spiritual suggestion:

Recall an experience in your life that seemed tragic at first, but from which positive things occurred. Thank God for these gifts.

God's Word:

I am afflicted and in pain;
let your saving help protect me, God.
That I may praise God's name in song
and glorify it with thanksgiving.

PSALM 69:30–31

DAY 26

Priorities

Every year I make a four-day retreat at the Trappist monastery south of Rochester, New York.

The monks there retire about 7:00 p.m. but rise at 2:25 a.m. to sing psalms. They seldom speak, eat meatless meals, and pray together seven times daily.

Most never leave the 2,500 acre monastery and are buried in a simple cemetery with only a plain wooden cross as a marker.

But to support the monastery they also weekly bake 50,000 loaves of Monk's Bread for their customers in nearby cities. Moreover, they radiate deep joy and serenity.

The first day at the abbey usually is a shock to my system, which is so used to noise and busyness. The retreat also challenges me. But, gradually, a serenity sweeps over my soul and I leave with a heart at peace and my spirit uplifted.

However, the atmosphere and the monks' example prompt these questions: Is God and God's word the first priority of my life? Am I ready for eternity?

Spiritual suggestion:

Ask yourself: Are God and God's Word the top priorities in my life? Am I ready for eternity?

God's Word:

The promises of the LORD are sure,
silver refined in a crucible,
silver purified seven times.

PSALM 12:7

Prayer of Pure Love

Here is a story about prayer:

A young girl loved her grandfather very much. She often called him purely out of love for the man.

Her phone calls greatly pleased the grandfather. A wealthy person, he decided to set up a savings account for his granddaughter, but without her knowing about it.

Every time she called, the grandfather deposited $1,000 into that account.

This little girl had reached twenty-three when the grandfather died. As the lawyer read the will, the young woman, to her surprise and shock, discovered that she was a multimillionaire.

Our prayer ideally should be out of pure love for God. But even if it isn't, God still responds more generously than that grandfather did.

Spiritual suggestion:

While prayers of asking, thanking, and repenting are pleasing to God, prayers of pure love and praise have special merit.

God's Word:

I will praise you, Lord, with all my heart;
I will declare all your wondrous deeds.
I will delight and rejoice in you;
I will sing hymns to your name, Most High.

PSALM 9:2–3

A Groom's Hopes

A groom recently expressed these dreams to his bride:

"Just looking at you, it would have been easy for anyone to fall for your outer beauty as I did. But it wasn't until I got to know you better that I realized that as beautiful as you are on the outside, it only scratched the surface of the person you are on the inside.

"Every night before I go to sleep, I kneel by my bedside to pray and thank God for all the great gifts I receive each day, and I especially thank God for you. I thank God for the woman you are and the wife and mother I know you will become, but most of all, I thank God for bringing you into my life. I pray that God will give me the strength and wisdom to be a good husband and father. I also pray that God will someday bless us with children so that we may share in the joys that our parents and all parents share."

It seems that the closer spouses are to God the closer they are to one another. And the closer they are to one another the closer they are to God.

Spiritual suggestion:

God's love for us is a model for spouses; conversely, the love between spouses is a reflection or indication of that divine love.

God's Word:

Happy are all who fear the LORD,
who walk in the ways of God.
What your hands provide you will enjoy;
you will be happy and prosper:
Like a fruitful vine
your wife within your home,
Like olive plants
your children around the table.
Just so will they be blessed
who fear the LORD.
May the LORD bless you from Zion,
all the days of your life
That you may share Jerusalem's joy
and live to see your children's children.
Peace upon Israel!

PSALM 128

DAY 29

Prayer after Attack on America

At a concert with the Syracuse Symphony shortly after September 11, 2001, singer Maureen McGovern recalled an incident with her grandfather during World War II.

Her dad flew large transport planes at great risk behind enemy lines during the invasion. Back home, her grandfather, every night, wrote his son a letter. Each one ended the same way: "Good night. Good luck. God bless."

McGovern also talked about the composer who wrote a famous song during World War I, when Americans longed for peace.

Later, before World War II, as we worried about the days ahead, the composer added this introduction to that same song: "Let us all be grateful for a land so fair, as we raise our voices in a solemn prayer."

The composer was Irving Berlin. The song, of course, "God Bless America."

She sang the prayer that night, as did many Americans after the Twin Tower tragedy.

Spiritual suggestion:

Think of troubled areas in the world and pray for peace with justice in those places.

God's Word:

You answer us with awesome deeds of justice,
O God our savior,
The hope of all the ends of the earth
and of far distant islands.

PSALM 65:6

When the Dying Speak

Dawn Green was only fifty, but, dying of cancer, she looked eighty.

Her husband Ron was preparing for another difficult night by his wife's side. She would often interrupt his sleep with questions or with comments about the voices speaking to her.

This night was no exception. At one point, she awakened him and said:

"Ron, I am worried. I don't know how I am going to get from here to there."

"Where is there?" he asked.

"Heaven, of course."

The next day Ron came from work at noon to prepare her lunch. Instead of a worried face, she displayed a radiant smile.

Dawn explained to a puzzled husband this shift in her attitude:

"Ron, you know those people and voices who have been around me? They all are on a bus. They said they have a ticket for me and I can join them on the bus.

The destination of that bus, Ron thought, read "Heaven Bound."

Dawn peacefully left her home on earth a few days later, riding that bus to her new home in heaven.

Spiritual suggestion:

Listening with love to those who are seriously ill always comforts them, and can inspire us as well.

God's Word:

O Most High, when I am afraid,
in you I place my trust.

PSALM 56:3–4

Dedication

The West Point Academy Glee Club visited Syracuse in the Fall of 2002, joining the Syracuse Symphony in a concert honoring veterans.

They were impressive in their uniforms, in their standing perfectly still at attention on risers for nearly an hour, and in their diversity, since about a third of the cadets were female.

But these outstanding young men and women, carefully selected for nomination to West Point, paid a price for this journey to our city.

Before being permitted to tour with the Glee Club, they must satisfactorily complete their current academic courses, physical training, and military studies. In addition, of course, these future leaders of America need to squeeze many music rehearsals into their demanding time schedules.

Such discipline and determination seemed even more impressive than their external appearance.

Spiritual suggestion:

Consider how we must pay a price for excellence in any endeavor.

God's Word:

One thing God has said;
two things I have heard:
Power belongs to God;
so too, Lord, does kindness,
And you render to each of us
according to our deeds.

PSALM 62:12–13

Half-Full or Half-Empty

Here is an old saying: When people look at a partially filled glass, some will say the glass is half-empty; others will say it is half-full.

Our attitude can change the way we perceive reality.

Walking downtown the other day, I thought of that saying

Many of the leaves with beautiful colors were still clinging to the trees; others had fallen to the ground.

We could say: Oh, shoot! Summer is over and the terrible winter will soon be upon us.

Or we could say: What a magnificent scene! The Creator's beauty in the fall reminds us that God will be with us during the winter and in the spring will raise up new life, new flowers, new leaves.

It really depends upon how you look at it.

Spiritual suggestion:

Ask yourself: What generally is my basic
attitude toward life's experiences—positive
(half-full) or negative (half-empty)?

God's Word:

I will call upon you; answer me, O God.
Turn your ear to me; hear my prayer.
Show your wonderful love,
you who deliver with your right arm
those who seek refuge from their foes.

PSALM 17:6–7

DAY 33

Thanksgiving

The Pilgrims, as we now say, got it right when they celebrated the first Thanksgiving Day. They counted their blessings and thanked God for them.

Today most Americans follow their example. We remember our gifts on Thanksgiving and thank the Lord for them.

Several special activities make our 9:30 Thanksgiving Day morning celebration at the cathedral quite popular.

Instead of the usual sermon or homily we spend a few minutes silently, but with musical background, gratefully reflecting on blessings of the past year.

Each member of every family brings an item or two of food for the poor to the altar.

We hand out a large loaf of bread, blessed during the service, to every household as they leave the cathedral and return to their homes.

We hope this connects the grateful celebration at church with a grateful celebration at home.

Spiritual suggestion:

Today, give thanks to God for three particular
blessings you have received.

God's Word:

It is good to give thanks to the LORD,
to sing praise to your name, Most High,
To proclaim your love in the morning,
your faithfulness in the night. . . .

PSALM 92:2–3

Truth, Goodness, and Beauty

The ancient philosopher Plato said that beauty attracts us, arrests us, and leads us beyond to something more.

Medieval philosophers extended his teaching. They taught that in addition to beauty, goodness and truth also engage us and lead us beyond. We witness this in everyday life.

A student finally solves a math problem and experiences the joy and serenity of experiencing truth.

We find our hearts warmed by another's good deed and feel inspired to imitate this example of goodness.

A beautiful sunset, fall foliage, or the ground pure white with fresh snow takes our breath away and lifts our spirits.

Those medieval philosophers argue further that truth, goodness, and beauty lead us to God, the source of all truth, goodness, and beauty.

Spiritual suggestion:

Let your memory recall an occasion when you solved a problem, witnessed the good deed of another, or experienced the beauty of nature. Then praise the God of truth, goodness, and beauty.

God's Word:

Praise the LORD, my soul;
I shall praise the LORD all my life,
sing praise to my God while I live.
                    PSALM 146:2

Forgiving and Reconnecting Before Death

The hospice chaplain asked Carl if he wished to pray for anyone or anything special.

Carl replied: "That the Lord take good care of my girls. And that Freddie and I can go around on the carousel.

Freddie and the carousel puzzled everyone.

Then they recalled that Carl's first marriage ended in a disaster and that afterwards Carl had little contact with his son, Freddie, born of this marriage. Later he married again to a woman with two daughters. He deeply loved and cared for those two girls.

Realizing Carl's desire now to reconnect with his son, someone called Freddie on a cell phone. He and his father then spoke for an hour.

Carl asked Freddie's forgiveness for the neglect of his son. Freddie asked forgiveness for neglecting his ailing father.

Forty-eight hours later, Carl died a peaceful death.

Spiritual suggestion:

We all have a person whom we have not forgiven and with whom we are not connected. Now is the moment to forgive that person and, if possible, reconnect.

God's Word:

Cleanse me with hyssop, that I may be pure; wash me, make me whiter than snow.

PSALM 51:9

Empowering Love

Dustin Hoffman is a talented actor, but also a temperamental perfectionist.

When filming the movie *Midnight Cowboy* with Jon Voight, the director had scheduled a difficult, emotional scene for late in the afternoon.

Such scenes require great effort and Hoffman, weary at this hour of the day, felt empty with his supply of needed energy depleted.

Jon Voight, noticing that Hoffman seemed agitated, asked what was the matter?

Hoffman grumbled about the director and his timing of the scene.

Voight touched his arm and said, "Dustin, you are great, you can do it, now do it."

And he did, an Academy Award winning performance.

Later Hoffman remarked: Jon Voight gave me a love tap; he unleashed my potential.

Spiritual suggestion:

By a pat on the back, some words of encouragement, or a specific compliment, empower someone to use her or his talents.

God's word:

How good it is, how pleasant,
where the people dwell as one!

PSALM 133:1

Self-Giving

Pope John Paul II is no stranger to self-giving.

He grew up in Poland under oppression, first by German Nazis and then by Russian Communists.

Later, as head of the Catholic Church, he suffered an assassin's bullet, made countless exhausting trips around the world bringing his message to others, and now daily carries the burden of deteriorating health.

When this pope teaches that only self-giving will give us contented hearts, he speaks from experience.

Every Christmas or birthday gift we give or receive is, or at least should be, an experience of self-giving love.

Thinking about that should further warm our hearts when we open those cards or unwrap a special present, or when we choose a card or gift for someone else.

Spiritual suggestion:

When you give or receive a gift, remember that self-giving love is, or should be, behind it.

God's Word:

Turn from evil and do good;
seek peace and pursue it.

PSALM 34:15

Abraham

The December 2001 cover story of *National Geographic* carried this title: "Abraham, the Father of Three Faiths."

Jewish people consider Abraham as the great patriarch, the one who, with trust, left home for an unknown land, who believed God's word about him and Sara having a son despite their old age, and who was willing to sacrifice his only child.

Christians consider themselves as descendants of Abraham. In our own Cathedral we have a century-old stained glass window of Abraham and often recite a prayer acknowledging that Abraham is our "father in faith."

Muslims view Abraham as one of God's great messengers. During their pilgrimage to Mecca they experience several rituals that recall incidents in the life of Abraham.

If people of these three faiths knew better each other's common reverence for Abraham, perhaps they could love one another more. And then there would be a greater chance for peace on earth.

Spiritual suggestion:

Reflect on the reverence for Abraham that Christian, Jewish, and Muslim people share.

God's Word:

Love and truth will meet;
justice and peace will kiss.
PSALM 85:11

Starting Over

Julie, a young woman on the West Coast, was pursuing a doctorate in psychology and considered herself an agnostic, a person with doubts about God and spiritual realities.

She was, however, intrigued with the Catholic Church and sought out a priest to talk with him about something that had happened to her ten years earlier.

She cautioned the cleric: "I don't want absolution, because I don't believe in confession and I don't want counseling, because I am a professional therapist.

After she had discussed the decade old incident, this priest wisely remarked:

"Sometimes, when we have made bad choices we cannot undo the harm done or make up for those poor decisions. But that is O.K., because it makes us rely totally upon God for forgiveness and strength."

What great advice when we want to start over and make a new beginning.

Spiritual suggestion:

If a dark part of your past plagues you, let it go and depend totally upon God for mercy and strength.

God's Word:

Have mercy on me, God,
have mercy on me.
In you I seek shelter.
In the shadow of your wings I seek shelter
till harm pass by.
I call to God Most High,
to God who provides for me.

PSALM 57:2–3

Giving Kids a Chance

When Sister Mary Jane became principal at our K–grade 6, center city Cathedral School a decade ago, only one of the dozen sixth-grade graduates finished high school. The rest just dropped out, victims of the culture, the environment, and even their backgrounds, since most came from below poverty-level households. For the past five years, our Guardian Angel Society Endowment Fund has provided scholarships for those graduates who wanted to attend a particular private junior or senior high school. We asked the institution to match that grant and the parents to pay the affordable difference.

Melanie was one of the initial beneficiaries. In her fourth year at the scholastically tough Christian Brothers Academy, she wrote: "I am a sophomore this year and I am doing excellent in my academic studies. I have a grade point average of about ninety-five. I am currently involved in Youth Group, Multicultural Club, Math Team, Spanish Club, Yearbook, and Student Senate. In the spring, I also participate in Varsity Track and Field. I wrote this letter to express my complete gratitude for your financial support. Without you I would not be able to attend this great place of education."

Her excellent record has continued and as a result several Ivy League colleges have recruited Melanie as a future student in their schools.

Many people combined to give Melanie this chance to break the cycle of poverty and, some day, make a unique contribution for the betterment of our world

Spiritual suggestion:

Are you making significant contributions of time, talents, or finances to programs that help give young people like Melanie a better chance in life?

God's Word:

Neither in my youth, nor now in old age
have I ever seen the just abandoned
or their children begging bread.
The just always lend generously,
and their children become a blessing.

PSALM 37:25–26

Try God

Every Saturday night, we offer Mass for about forty ambulatory residents at a local nursing home near Syracuse University. Afterwards, a corps of visitors brings Communion to those unable to leave their rooms.

I was asked to speak with a fifty-year-old, seriously ill man who had been admitted to that nursing home several days earlier.

We had never met before.

After a preliminary greeting, he asked:

"What's your name?"

"Father Champlin."

"Are you on the radio?"

"Yes, I do some radio spots every week."

He replied with a spark of recognition:

"If you have tried everything else, why not try God. Right?"

"Right!"

Wow, I thought to myself afterwards. Without realizing it, these spiritual suggestions are giving hope to some people who are really struggling.

"You may have tried everything else; why not try God?" is, as I mentioned at the beginning of this book, the tag line at the end of each radio spot. Its frequent repetition over the airwaves for nearly two years clearly has impacted some people.

Spiritual suggestion:

Identify someone close to you who has tried everything else, and pray that this person will try God.

God's Word:

Listen, God, to my prayer;
do not hide from my pleading;
hear me and give answer.

PSALM 55:2–3

Deathless Love

Sullivan Ballou, a young Providence, Rhode Island lawyer with a promising political future, enlisted in the army at the outbreak of the Civil War.

From a camp near Washington, he wrote a letter to his wife beginning "My very dear Sarah."

In that note Ballou exclaimed: "Sarah, my love for you is deathless. It seems to bind me with mighty cables that nothing but omnipotence could break. . . ."

He continued, "The memories of the blissful moments I have spent with you come creeping over me, and I feel most gratified to God and to you that I have enjoyed them so long."

Aware that he might perish in battle, Ballou added: "O Sarah! If the dead can come back to this earth and flit unseen around those they loved, I shall always be near you; in the gladdest days and darkest nights . . . always, always. . . ."

"Sarah, do not mourn me dead; think I am gone and wait for thee, for we shall meet again."

Sullivan Ballou died in battle one month later at Bull Run.

Spiritual suggestion:

That example of a husband's great love for his spouse and country should warm our hearts and inspire us to imitate this kind of love.

God's Word:

LORD, you have been our refuge
through all generations.
Before the mountains were born,
the earth and the world brought forth,
from eternity to eternity you are God.
A thousand years in your eyes
are merely a yesterday.

PSALM 90:1–2

Serving Others

A local advertising firm decided this year not to send gifts to its clients. Instead, they used those funds to host a Christmas party for some at-risk children.

They selected our boys and girls at Cathedral School, most of whom, as noted before, come from below poverty-level-income households, to be beneficiaries of their decision.

It was a great four-hour celebration starting around 10:00 that morning at the school.

All team members of the advertising firm participated. They served chicken wings and pizza; they dished out ice cream for the kids to make their own sundaes; they painted faces, told stories, and sang Christmas carols with the youngsters.

The children's joy in receiving was very obvious. One little boy told his mother that this was the best day of his life.

But the adults' joy in giving also was evident.

Spiritual suggestion:

The Bible tells us that there is more joy in giving than in receiving. (Acts 20:35)

God's Word:

Come, let us sing joyfully to the LORD;
cry out to the rock of our salvation.
Let us greet him with a song of praise,
joyfully sing out our psalms.

PSALM 95:1–2

Wants and Needs

I recently had dinner with four married couples in their early thirties.

My question to them: What are your current spiritual concerns?

Trying to keep their own family lives simple in the face of today's advertising was, for them, a major challenge. They said that the media, especially television, seemingly tries to transform our wants into needs. When their kids plead for something and are told that they don't really need the thing they want, the children counter with the fact that other kids already have it.

One of the couples, last Lent, put a cloth over the television set and decided not to watch TV through that season. It was, they said, hard at first. But they soon discovered at home freer conversations, better communication, and greater involvement in family oriented games.

And a clearer view of wants and needs.

Spiritual suggestion:

Spend a few moments distinguishing between some of your wants and your actual needs.

God's Word:

The LORD is my shepherd;
there is nothing I lack.
In green pastures you let me graze;
to safe waters you lead me;
you restore my strength.
You guide me along the right path
for the sake of your name.
Even when I walk through a dark valley,
I fear no harm for you are at my side;
your rod and staff give me courage.
You set a table before me
as my enemies watch;
You anoint my head with oil;
my cup overflows.
Only goodness and love will pursue me
all the days of my life;
I will dwell in the house of the LORD
for years to come.

PSALM 23

DAY 45

Fasting and Self-denial

For Christians, Lent is a time to pray, fast, and serve others.

Many freely choose to give up for these 40 days something they like or enjoy. Such acts of self-denial help us become more disciplined, prepare our hearts for Easter, and better appreciate people in need.

Jewish people similarly fast and practice self-denial, especially at the time of Yom Kippur.

Muslims likewise spend the entire month of Ramadan in a very strict fast. Each day they have nothing to eat or drink from sun up to sun down.

Fasting and self-denial helps us focus on divine realities and keep our priorities straight here on earth.

Spiritual suggestion:

Do you value occasional voluntary acts of self-denial and practice them?

God's Word:

I have made vows to you, God;
with offerings I will fulfill them,
Once you have snatched me from death,
kept my feet from stumbling,
That I may walk before God
in the light of the living.

PSALM 56:13–14

Lent

The teenager walked into high school wearing a black, ashen cross on her forehead.

A friend inquired: "Did you forget to wash your face this morning?"

"No, I just came from church for Ash Wednesday."

Her friend responded: "What is Ash Wednesday?"

"Ash Wednesday is the beginning of Lent."

The still puzzled friend asked, "What is Lent?"

It seems that we can no longer expect that all Americans understand long-standing Christian traditions.

Lent is for followers of Christ, a period of forty days of preparing for Easter.

They pray a little bit more.

They fast or give up something they like.

They try to serve others better, doing something extra for persons in need.

The more serious Christians are about Lent, the deeper will be their joy at Easter.

Spiritual suggestion:

Special religious seasons like Lent are
opportunities for drawing closer to God. We
can also set aside days, or add practices such
as you are by praying with this book, as a way
to draw closer to God at any time of year.

God's Word:

Turn from evil and do good,
that you may inherit the land forever.
PSALM 37:27

Olympics

On that Friday night when the Olympic games opened in Salt Lake City, I was fatigued from a long flight, and weary from a lengthy illness—not really in the mood to be inspired by anything.

But the colorful and remarkable procession of contestants from so many nations at the opening ceremony just pushed aside all my fatigue and weariness.

At a time of global animosity and divisions, here were thousands of mostly young people from diverse backgrounds bonded together as one.

These youthful men and women were filled with life and enthusiasm.

Their smiles radiated joy.

Our God is a God of love, life, and joy. Was I discerning the presence of God in Salt Lake City on that Friday night?

Spiritual suggestion:

Reflect on this great truth: Joy is the inevitable sign of God's presence.

God's Word:

Send your light and fidelity,
that they may be my guide
And bring me to your holy mountain,
to the place of your dwelling,
That I may come to the altar of God,
to God, my joy, my delight.
Then I will praise you with the harp,
O God, my God.

PSALM 43:3–4

DAY 48

Solitude and Silence

I grew up as a teenager on the north shore of Oneida Lake near Cleveland, New York, a small town with approximately five hundred residents. Each morning around 6:30 I walked about a mile or so to catch the school bus for Camden High School, some eleven miles away. Since these were World War II gas rationing days, I often had to hitchhike home over those nearly dozen miles after finishing soccer, basketball, and baseball practice. That uncertain mode of travel sometimes entailed long periods of anxious waiting for a friendly driver or even walking a few of the miles, when necessary.

I consequently spent many adolescent hours in solitude and silence.

But those lengthy moments alone also enriched me with sights, sounds, and smells I could otherwise have missed: spectacular sunrises, birds chirping, and fresh mown fields of hay.

There were likewise times when I quietly spoke to God and God spoke to me.

Solitude and silence seem essential for a solid spiritual life.

Spiritual suggestion:

Try to spend some quiet time alone. Solitude and silence can enable us to experience reflections and insights we might otherwise miss.

God's Word:

Praise, you servants of the LORD,
praise the name of the LORD.
Blessed be the name of the LORD
both now and forever.
From the rising of the sun to its setting
let the name of the LORD be praised.

PSALM 113:1–3

Forgiveness of Others

The novel *A Bend in the Road*, by best-selling author Nicholas Sparks, centers around two people, both of whom need to forgive other people.

Sarah Andrews, college graduate and school teacher, learned after several years of marriage that for physical reasons she would be unable to bear a child. Her husband, upon hearing this, rejected Sarah and soon sought a divorce.

Miles Riley lost his wife and the mother of their young son two years earlier when a hit and run driver struck his wife who was jogging in the twilight along a country road.

Sparks describes the long and painful journeys of Sarah and Miles as they struggle to forgive and let go.

Every person can easily identify someone who, in a major or minor way, has hurt her or him in the past. That requires forgiving and letting go—essential elements for peace.

Spiritual suggestion:

Mentioning by name in prayer someone who has wounded us in the past may very well be the most effective tool for helping us to forgive and let go.

God's Word:

For day and night your hand was heavy upon me;
my strength withered as in dry summer heat.
Then I declared my sin to you;
my guilt I did not hide.
I said, 'I confess my faults to the LORD,'
and you took away the guilt of my sin.

PSALM 32:5

My Sickness

During my first 45 years as a priest, I was blessed with remarkably high energy and unusually good health. As I began my 46th year in the priesthood, all of that changed.

The initial shadow appeared at a Memorial Day 5K race when, for the first time in 30 years of running, I had to stop twice out of fatigue and was exhausted at the end.

The dark cloud arrived last October, when an ugly dry cough and deep weariness would not go away.

After many tests, the physician announced his bad news/good news findings:

The bad news: I now had Waldenstrom's disease, a low grade but incurable lymphoma found in the bone marrow.

The good news: It is the least aggressive of cancers and most easily treatable.

It seemed that I then needed to begin practicing in my own life the message I had been proclaiming over the radio during the previous year:

"You may have tried everything else; why not try God?"

Spiritual suggestion:

Recall how you have dealt with sickness in your life, especially of the serious type. Did you turn to God?

God's Word:

When the just cry out, the LORD hears
and rescues them from all distress.

PSALM 34:18

DAY 51

Evoking Smiles and Prompting Gratitude

I stop at the Carousel Mall about twice a week between 8:00 and 9:00 in the evening. The trips there are to take advantage of its fine post office, whose hours parallel those of the huge mall itself. That late closing time often works well for me.

The main entrance facing Onondaga Lake is always a busy place and is especially so during pre-holiday times.

The doors present a lighthearted challenge for me. I make a point to hold a door open for those coming or going and then await the response.

Some just pass right through without a word or look.

Most mumble "thanks."

Still others seem sort of stunned, then break into a smile, and utter an enthusiastic "thank you."

This door holding is my small effort to bring smiles and gratitude into our stress-filled world.

Spiritual suggestion:

Offer a smile and a thoughtful deed to a stranger and see if these acts of kindness prompt a return smile or grateful word.

God's Word:

Why are you downcast, my soul;
Why do you groan within me?
Wait for God, whom I shall praise again,
my savior and my God.

PSALM 43:5

Blessings in Burdens

Early on a Sunday morning, I opened the church and discovered a monstrous mess of broken glass all over the sanctuary.

A large spotlight suspended from the ceiling 90 feet above had torn loose and crashed onto the altar.

It was a burdensome task to clean up swiftly, before Mass began, countless shattered pieces of glass scattered around the sanctuary.

Later I realized what a blessing it was that this crash happened in the darkness of the night and not in the middle of the service. Had it occurred otherwise, someone could have been killed (perhaps me) and many seriously injured.

Teddy Roosevelt, as a young member of the New York State legislature, passionately wanted to be elected its Speaker and earnestly campaigned for the position. His election seemed certain, but opposing political forces entered the picture and another person was chosen.

At first Roosevelt felt chagrined and depressed by this sudden negative turn of events. Then his mood improved. He realized the burden was really a blessing and that he could actually accomplish much more than if he had been elected Speaker.

Spiritual suggestion:

Recall an experience in your life in which a
burden proved to be a blessing in disguise.

God's Word:

How lovely your dwelling,
O LORD of hosts!
My soul yearns and pines
for the courts of the LORD.
My heart and flesh cry out
for the living God.
As the swallow finds a home
and the swallow a nest to settle her young,
My home is by your altars,
LORD of hosts, my king and my God!

PSALM 84:2–4

Racism

In 1901, during the first days of his administration, Theodore Roosevelt did something no other president had done: he invited a black man to dinner in the White House.

His guest was Booker T. Washington, head of the Tuskegee Institute in Alabama, and then the most powerful black man in America.

It was a quiet event, with only the president, his wife, and another person joining them. At 2:00 a.m., however, an Associated Press reporter sent a dispatch through the nation simply stating that, "Booker T. Washington dined with the President last evening."

Many praised this breakthrough, but others reacted violently. A Memphis paper called it "a damnable outrage that the President invited a nigger to dine with him at the White House."

Such gross racism in the past stunned me. But we surely must deal with more subtle forms of prejudice today.

Spiritual suggestion:

Can you identify any racism or prejudice around you or within your own heart?

God's Word:

Why, LORD, do you stand at a distance
and pay no heed to these troubled times?

PSALM 10:1

DAY 54

Suffering and Evil in the World

A man around forty, an airline pilot, whom I have known since he was a youngster, sent me a note of support during my own illness. He wrote:

"It is times like these that I have difficulty understanding God's grand scheme of things."

"Why is it," he asked, "that individuals of evil or malicious character remain relatively unscathed as they progress through life?"

"Yet it seems," he continued, "the good and virtuous of this life are burdened with the pain and suffering!"

His conclusion was: "I suppose it is all part of the great mystery of existence."

Some Christians find the answer to that age-old question of "Why me, God?" or just "Why, God?" by reflecting on the cross. They see here a good and innocent man suffering and dying out of love for others, for us.

Spiritual suggestion:

Gaze upon a crucifix or cross as you reflect upon some suffering or evil you have experienced.

God's Word:

My God, my God, why have you abandoned me?
Why so far from my call for help,
from my cries of anguish?
My God, I call by day, but you do not answer;
by night, but I have no relief.

PSALM 22:2–3

Exaggerated Self-Importance

Christian Herter, the Governor of Massachusetts, had been campaigning all day, but with nothing to eat. He thus looked forward to the final stop at a fund-raising chicken barbecue.

As he held out his tray for the chicken, the woman server placed one piece on his plate.

Half-starved, the governor asked, "May I have another piece of chicken?"

"No," the lady replied, "only one per person."

"But, ma'am," Herter pleaded, "I haven't had anything all day. Would you please give me another piece?"

"No," she insisted, "only one piece per person."

Now annoyed, he decided to exert his power. "Ma'am, do you know who I am? I am Christian Herter, the governor of this state."

After an awkward silent pause, the lady responded: "Do you know who I am? I am the woman who serves one piece of chicken per person at this barbecue."

Spiritual suggestion:

It is good for us not to get too puffed up or take ourselves too seriously.

God's Word:

LORD, my heart is not proud;
nor are my eyes haughty.
I do not busy myself with great matters,
with things too sublime for me.
Rather, I have stilled my soul,
hushed it like a weaned child.
Like a weaned child on its mother's lap,
so is my soul within me.
Israel, hope in the LORD,
now and forever.
PSALM 131:1–3

A Shared Sacred Place

Many complex and deep-seated differences are behind the frightening hatred and violence in the Holy Land.

However, the defiant visit of a Jewish leader to the Muslim Dome of the Rock some time ago seemed to trigger the current clashes.

How sad. Here is a place, sacred to Christians, Jews, and Muslims, that has become a source of bitter division rather than a basis for peaceful co-existence.

This masterpiece known as the Dome of the Rock was built on a location significant to all three religions.

For Christians, it is considered the site of Jesus' ascension to heaven.

For Jews, it was the location of Solomon's now destroyed magnificent temple.

For Muslims, the Dome has been erected over the rock from which they believe Muhammed made his night journey to heaven.

Spiritual suggestion:

Pray for the day when believers from these three major religious traditions might worship in peace at this shared sacred place in Jerusalem.

God's Word:

Streams of the river gladden the city of God,
the holy dwelling of the Most High.
God is in its midst; it shall not be shaken;
God will help it at break of day.

PSALM 46:5–6

Starting Over

I have always loved spring.

The days are longer and the weather warmer.

Trees suddenly sprout beautiful leaves, and seeds planted in the ground emerge as living plants.

The grass grows rapidly and birds start chirping at daylight.

The darkness and death of winter have yielded to the light and life of spring.

Spring gives most people an emotional lift. But it also can give us a spiritual lesson.

The lesson is about letting go, starting over, beginning again.

As a lover of sports, I learned over the years that the best athletes are those who do not rest on their laurels or fret over their mistakes. They do not reflect upon a great play or brood over a bad one. They simply move on to the next challenge.

Spring and sports can teach us how to live our lives, by letting go, starting over, and beginning again.

Spiritual suggestion:

Ask yourself: Do I have a constant and unhealthy tendency to rest upon my laurels or fret over my mistakes instead of moving on?

God's Word:

Whenever I lay down and slept,
the LORD preserved me to rise again.

PSALM 3:6

Raising Funds for Good Causes

My promise for the Memorial Day 5K run was this: I will begin the race and finish it either by jogging or walking, in a wheelchair, or by ambulance.

Before the training started, an orthopedic specialist did an x-ray on my knees and found them better than ever for a seventy-two-year-old man.

However, since I had not run for six months because of cancer, the physician gave me strict guidelines for re-entry: Heat up the knee beforehand and ice it afterwards. Start with a half-mile and gradually extend it. Do no more than two days in a row. And if the knee hurts, call him immediately.

The race was for fun, but it was also a fund-raiser for our kids at Cathedral School, most of whom are from below poverty-level income homes.

The monies donated help us give these kids a chance at life, a way out of poverty and the possibility of being productive members of the community.

I did finish the race, but only by alternately jogging and fast walking. My time was five minutes slower than previous years, but we did raise $45,000 for the boys and girls of our school.

Spiritual suggestion:

Try to participate annually in one or several
fund-raising activities for good causes.

God's Word:

The earth has yielded its harvest;
God, our God, blesses us. . . .
Who gives a home for the forsaken,
who leads prisoners out to prosperity. . . .
PSALM 67:7–68:7

A Shaky Self-Image

Some people maintain that as human beings we inherit a subtle and unconscious, but real, tendency not to care deeply about ourselves. This trend results in shaky self-images.

In support of their theory, they pose a few questions for us:

How well do I take compliments?

Do I pick at myself, pointing out the flaws in an otherwise fairly perfect effort?

Am I able, comfortably, to receive love from other people?

Do I have a more than usual need to be recognized, affirmed, and praised?

In a confrontation of some significance, do I tend to be aggressive, passive, or assertive?

Am I struggling with any severe addiction?

Our answers can be quite revealing.

However, the real basis for a sound, healthy, and positive self-image is recognizing that God unconditionally loves each one of us.

Spiritual suggestion:

Consider your own answers to these questions, and try to accept God's unconditional love.

God's Word:

Learn to savor how good the LORD is. . . .
The LORD is close to the brokenhearted,
saves those whose spirit is crushed.
PSALM 34:9, 19

DAY 60

Providential Coincidences

I took the train to New York to meet with my brother Chuck. He and his wife had come from Los Angeles to the Big Apple for a meeting. We were to get together for a nice dinner at a fine restaurant and catch up on our lives. Although we had talked often on the phone after my cancer had been diagnosed five months earlier, this was the first time I had seen my brother and his spouse since then.

Soon after checking into the hotel, the phone rang. It was my sister-in-law telling me that upon leaving a luncheon session, Chuck had fallen, fracturing his hip and wrist, and causing an ugly laceration on his forehead and a closed black eye.

He was still in the Emergency Department at St. Claire's Hospital, but soon would be moved to an upstairs room.

I walked the few blocks to the hospital, and was able to spend an hour with my badly bruised, legally blind brother. Before catching the train back the next morning, I saw him again.

Our anticipated pleasant get-together turned into something quite different. But what a providential coincidence that I was there by his side at a dark moment.

Spiritual suggestion:

See if you can recall a coincidence in which,
under God's loving care, something dark has
a bright dimension to it.

God's Word:

But you, LORD, are a shield around me;
my glory, you keep my head high.

PSALM 3:4

Tithing Time and Treasure

The teenager shouted to his dad, "You are stupid!"

The father, Jim Kelly, responded: "I know, son, but what makes you say that now?"

His boy replied: "Saturday morning is the only day you can sleep in and every week instead you get up and go to a dumb 7:00 meeting."

The father's dumb meeting is actually a weekly prayer session with about a half-dozen men.

A native of Ohio, Kelly graduated from Yale and accepted a position in Charlotte, North Carolina working with the homeless and with addicts. Later he became a church development director.

Jim and his wife tithe, sharing that 10 percent of their finances with the church and the poor.

Jim also spends 5 percent of his time continuing, but as a volunteer, those efforts with the homeless.

His son's comments were probably more in admiration than in criticism of his devout father.

Spiritual suggestion:

Examine your lifestyle to determine if you share 10 percent of your income with a church and the poor and a similar portion of your time in volunteer service of others?

God's Word:

For the LORD hears the poor,
does not spurn those in bondage.

PSALM 69:34

Caring for the Environment

Mayor Matthew Driscoll has a dream for the city of Syracuse, New York. His vision can be reduced to two words: Green and Clean.

Recently, he asked local residents to bring a broom and a bag to Clinton Square, this city's center, for the kickoff of a monthly program to clean up the downtown area.

About a century earlier, President Theodore Roosevelt was traveling down the Mississippi and came up with a similar dream and vision. He declared that we must preserve our natural resources, especially water and forests, for future generations. To accomplish this goal, he established some federal guidelines and agencies.

The efforts of the mayor and the president follow God's command in the Bible.

Having just created a very beautiful world, God ordered our ancestors "to cultivate and care for it" (Genesis 2). Today, God similarly commands us to be good caretakers of the world around us.

Spiritual suggestion:

Today, do one thing that in some way makes our world more beautiful.

God's Word:

The voice of the LORD is over the waters;
the God of glory thunders,
the LORD, over the mighty waters.
The voice of the LORD is power;
the voice of the LORD is splendor.

PSALM 29:3–4

The Nature of God

We can never fully understand the nature of God. But the rain, sun, and wind give us some ideas about what God is like.

Rain can be violent and destructive, but usually falls gently upon the earth. Its drops seem very careful not to hurt, but rather to help every living thing.

The sun shines upon all. There are no distinctions, no favoritism, no discrimination. It makes things grow, warms our bodies, and lifts our spirits.

The wind is invisible, but powerful. We can see leaves flutter, but not the wind that makes them do so. The wind pushes us along, creates energy, and points us in the right direction.

God likewise is gentle, has no favorites, and is invisible, but powerful.

Spiritual suggestion:

Reflect upon these connections between rain, sun, or wind and God.

God's Word:

I will praise you among the peoples, LORD;
I will chant your praise among the nations.
For your love towers to the heavens;
your faithfulness to the skies.
Show yourself over the heavens, God;
may your glory appear above all the earth.

PSALM 57:10–12

God's Will in Our Lives

Ann's husband and young daughter really wanted a dog. She, on the other hand, strongly opposed the idea.

Eventually, but reluctantly, Ann gave in. The family now has a puppy in the house.

As you might guess, Ann ended up with the task of taking the dog for a walk—every day, every morning and every night, at dawn and at dusk.

She resented the role at first. However, Ann soon discovered that it gave her a quiet time twice each day for peaceful reflection and silent prayer.

The walks have now become two treasured moments in her daily routine.

Spiritual suggestion:

Doing God's will frequently appears in the beginning to be a painful task or a burdensome duty. But eventually, we often experience totally unexpected benefits.

God's Word:

How good God is to the upright,
the LORD, to those who are clean of heart.

PSALM 73:1

Day 65

Excessive Self-Preoccupation

John is infatuated with Mary, but brokenhearted because of her. She recently rejected him, told him that their relationship was over, that she simply didn't love him any more.

Depressed by the rejection, he went for a walk in the woods to ponder this sad state of affairs.

It was one of those magnificent days and a particularly beautiful setting in which to enjoy the world of nature.

But John was so preoccupied with his heartache that he didn't even notice the flowers, the trees, or the spectacular sky. He missed all of the reality around him because of his excessive preoccupation with himself.

We may chuckle at the fate of that lovesick young man. But, like John, if we are unduly preoccupied with ourselves, we can miss much of God's richness that surrounds us.

Spiritual suggestion:

Can you recall a time when you missed something beautiful and special because you were preoccupied with another matter?

God's Word:

Look upon me, answer me, LORD, my God!
Give light to my eyes lest I sleep in death,
Lest my enemy say, 'I have prevailed,'
lest my foes rejoice at my downfall.

PSALM 13:4–5

Our Imperfections

The wise founders of our nation knew that all future citizens would be imperfect beings.

Aware of that, people like Alexander Hamilton, James Madison, and Thomas Jefferson established a government with three branches and a series of checks and balances that would keep imperfect people from misusing power.

An awareness of our imperfect human nature can help us in two ways.

First, that awareness should ease the disillusionment we feel when leaders of any type may let us down by their flawed conduct.

Secondly, that awareness should make us more compassionate toward the failings of others.

"Be compassionate," Jesus said, "as your heavenly Father is compassionate."

Spiritual suggestion:

As you struggle to cope with the failings of a church or state leader, recall some of your own imperfections and be more gentle in your judgment.

God's Word:

Once I prayed, 'LORD, have mercy on me; heal me, I have sinned against you.'

PSALM 41

The Dark and Ugly; the Bright and Beautiful

In the midst of constant publicity about clergy abuse of children, I recently experienced first, the dark and ugly, and shortly thereafter, the bright and beautiful side of life.

A man walking down the mall corridor with his wife and young daughter spotted me with black suit and white collar moving in the opposite direction toward them.

He immediately spread his arms out defensively in front of spouse and child. That gesture said in effect: "I must protect my dear wife and little girl from this predatory priest."

It stunned me to realize that for him a priest is someone dark and ugly.

Several weeks later, on a flight from Harrisburg to Chicago, I was sitting in the aisle seat next to an older woman, who sat by the window.

We scarcely spoke with each other during the short trip, both preoccupied with our own matters.

However, as we deplaned, she turned and said: "The Lord told me to give this to you for someone in need." She then placed a $50 bill in my hand.

For her, a priest is still someone bright and beautiful.

Spiritual suggestion:

Pray today for those clergy who are flawed and have failed in living out their call, and for those who are faithful and have emerged victorious in the challenges of their vocation.

God's Word:

I waited, waited for the LORD;
who bent down and heard my cry,
Drew me out of the pit of destruction,
out of the mud of the swamp,
Set my feet upon rock,
steadied my steps,
And put a new song in my mouth,
a hymn to our God.
Many shall look on in awe
and they shall trust in the LORD.

PSALM 40:2–4

Learning From Painful Experiences

Secretary of State Colin Powell, as a young military officer, served during the early stages of war in Southeast Asia as an advisor to Vietnamese troops.

Getting the soldiers to wear protective vests was one of his tasks.

They resisted his recommendation. The vests were too hot and heavy for the climate.

After some of the soldiers fell to enemy fire, a few of the Vietnamese put on the vests.

Shortly thereafter, members of a patrol began giggling. The reason for the laughter: a lead soldier had stood up and turned around to point out the enemy's location. He was immediately shot in the back. However, the bullet only imbedded itself in the protective vest. A hot and heavy vest had saved the soldier's life.

The soldiers then became believers, and all regularly wore the protective vests, despite the inconvenience.

Isn't it sad that we usually learn lessons about life only after painful experiences?

Spiritual suggestion:

Consider an occasion in which you personally grew as a result of a painful experience or a bad choice on your part.

God's Word:

Teach me to do your will,
for you are my God.
May your kind spirit guide me
on ground that is level.

PSALM 143:10–11

Listening with Love

A counselor guarantees successful marriages to engaged couples, if they spend ten minutes every day of their married lives listening with love to each other.

His suggestion works this way:

The husband, for example, arrives home from a difficult day at work. However, putting aside his own preoccupations, he sits across from his wife, then looks upon her face, which communicates feelings, and into her eyes, which are the doorways to her soul.

"I love you very much," he says to his spouse. "Tell me about your day."

Next he listens with love for five minutes.

Now the roles reverse. She casts aside her own preoccupations, looks upon his face and into his eyes, saying, "I, too, love you very much. Tell me about your day."

Then she listens with love for five minutes.

The marriage expert predicts success for couples who follow this recommendation about listening with love each day.

Spiritual suggestion:

Make an effort today to listen with love to someone who seeks you out and clearly needs an attentive, caring ear.

God's Word:

Hear my voice, LORD, when I call;
have mercy on me and answer me.

PSALM 27:7

The Importance of Exercise

I have loved long-distance swimming ever since my earliest days.

It began as a kid living at Hammondsport, New York and swimming for hours each day in beautiful and clear Keuka Lake.

It continued as a teenager, when during summer months after working each day on the railroad as a section hand, I would ride my bike a mile to the sand mines east of Cleveland, New York. There I swam in the clear, but murky pond used for dredging commercial sand.

Over the past twenty years, I have been blessed to swim regularly in the pure, but cool waters of Skaneateles Lake, one of the six major Finger Lakes in Central New York, and one as clear and clean as Keuka Lake.

Whenever I plunge into that lake, my worries, tensions, and fatigue instantly dissolve. This experience echoes the advice of health care experts. Their research shows that frequent and regular exercise benefits us mentally, physically, and spiritually.

Spiritual suggestion:

Make some physical experience a frequent part of your daily routine.

God's Word:

All you peoples, clap your hands;
shout to God with joyful cries.
For the LORD, the Most High, inspires awe,
the great king over all the earth. . . .

PSALM 47:2–3

Day 71

Beauty of God's Creation

I spent a day off on a recent Thursday visiting the Thousand Islands, located in the St. Lawrence River as it passes between Northern New York and Canada.

On the journey north, I found the sky a lovely blue with scattered white clouds, the foliage wonderfully green, and the temperature perfect.

I arrived at the cottage of friends on the St. Lawrence River. There we had lunch, a short run, and a visit next to the ever-flowing river.

We then traveled down to Alexandria Bay for a celebration of their wedding anniversary at the splendid Jacques Cartier Room in the Riveredge Resort.

The meal was expensive, but superb, and the service quite superior. But the most significant part was a magnificent view of the river sparkling in the late afternoon sun, followed by a gorgeous sunset.

I drove back to Syracuse in the dark with a very contented heart and words from the psalms on my lips: "Oh Lord, our God, how wonderful are all your works."

Spiritual suggestion:

Make a conscious effort today to appreciate the beauty of nature and give grateful praise to the God of all creation.

God's Word:

How great are your works, LORD!
How profound your purpose!

PSALM 92:6

Adjusting

Both Catholics and Muslims use beads for their private prayer. The most common form for Roman Catholics is the rosary with its one bead for the Lord's Prayer and ten beads for the Hail Marys.

On a recent trip, I forgot my rosary beads. However, I did have an unusual number of coins in my pocket.

During the flight, I lowered the tray table, counted out ten pennies, and began praying the Hail Mary, moving each coin when I finished the prayer.

Since there are five decades—fifty Hail Marys—in the basic rosary, this prayer experience took about ten minutes.

As I was finishing my informal rosary, the curious flight attendant stopped, spotted the neatly laid out coins, and asked what new game I was playing.

My response quickly ended his questioning and he moved on.

Adjusting to adversity can lead us to creative efforts and sometimes surprising results.

Spiritual suggestion:

Recall instances in which you adjusted to adversity by some creative effort and even experienced surprising results.

God word:

I wait for you, O LORD;
I lift up my soul to my God.
In you I trust; do not let me be disgraced;
do not let my enemies gloat over me.
No one is disgraced who waits for you,
but only those who lightly break faith.

PSALM 25:1–3

Visitation of Prisoners

Match Two is a volunteer program in California, which links volunteers who agree to visit a prisoner and prisoners who agree to be visited.

The visitors accept the responsibility of calling upon the same prisoner once a month for a year. The Match Two organization provides ten hours of training and orientation before a visitor begins the visitation.

The prisoners to be visited are scheduled for potential release from prison in about a year, soon after the proposed twelve encounters. A Match Two leader interviews prisoners, obtains their consent to be visited, and then matches them up with a volunteer visitor.

The state correctional agency loves Match Two and welcomes the visitors. Long-term studies reveal that the rate of prisoners slipping back onto crime and returning to prison is much less for those who had Match Two visits than those who did not.

Here is a fascinating and successful carrying out of Jesus' words in Matthew 25: "I was in prison and you visited me."

Spiritual suggestion:

Ask yourself whether Christ's words about responding and not responding to the sick, hungry, naked, stranger, or imprisoned make you a bit uneasy or uncomfortable.

God's Word:

Attend, my people, to my teaching;
listen to the words of my mouth.

PSALM 78:1

Saying Our Good-Byes

Every day, Blaine Mayhugh kisses his wife good-bye before leaving for the afternoon shift at work. If his two children, ages 7 and 8, are around, he gives each of them a hug and kiss as well.

One day, however, his wife was mowing the lawn and he was late. So, instead of kissing her, he simply waved good-bye and shouted that he loved her.

Later, trapped 240 feet below ground in a Pennsylvania mine, the first thing he thought of was this failure to kiss his wife good-bye.

After the miraculous rescue following three days of entrapment, Mayhugh commented, "I didn't give her a kiss good-bye that day, and that's probably the only day I never did, to be honest with you."

Saying our good-byes, even for short-term separations, are significant experiences. Sending kids to school or bed, a spouse to work or on a trip may seem routine and ordinary events, but they are not; they all demand our loving, careful attention.

Spiritual suggestion:

Reflect on your own recent experiences of saying "Good-night" or "Good-bye." Were they merely routine or were you well aware of these as particularly significant moments?

God's Word:

In peace I shall both lie down and sleep, for you alone, LORD, make me secure.

PSALM 4:9

Praying for Help

An Amtrak train from Chicago to Washington, D.C., had almost reached the capitol when it derailed, sending several cars on their sides. Trapped inside one of them were three women passengers, two of whom seemed to be suffocating in the 120 degree heat.

A local firefighter crawled to where the women were and said, "Ladies, I'm fireman Mick McKenzie. We're in a bit of a predicament here."

After asking the names of each he went on: "Okay, here's what we are going to do. First off, we're going to start praying." They all held hands and prayed—a single basic prayer, nothing glamorous.

Then McKenzie told them: "I'm going to do everything in my power to get you guys out. I'm not going to leave you."

An hour later, the firefighter, with assistance from his colleagues, had brought them out of the crushed car and to safety.

Spiritual suggestion:

Praying for help in any circumstance is a praiseworthy thing to do.

God's Word:

In you, LORD, I take refuge;
let me never be put to shame.
In your justice deliver me;
incline your ear to me;
make haste to rescue me!

PSALM 31:2–3

Being Grateful and Not Complaining

The Cottage Café Restaurant at Bethany Beach along the Delaware Shore places on the center of each table a series of cards describing drinks and desserts plus an inspirational one entitled "When I Whine."

That motivational message goes like this:

Today, upon a bus, I saw a girl with golden hair.
And wished I was as fair.

When suddenly she rose to leave, I saw her hobble down the aisle.

She had one leg and wore a crutch.

But as she passed, a smile.

Oh, God, forgive me when I whine.

I have two legs, the world is mine.

Later, while walking down the street, I saw a child with eyes of blue.

He stood and watched the others play.

He did not know what to do.

I stopped a moment and then I said,

"Why don't you join the others, dear?"

He looked ahead without a word.

And then I knew, he couldn't hear.

Oh God, forgive me when I whine.

I have two ears, the world is mine.

With feet to take me where I'd go.

With ears to hear what I'd know.

Oh, God, forgive me when I whine.

Spiritual suggestion:

Bring to mind a past encounter with someone who was blind, crippled, deaf, or in some other way less fortunate; did you find it curbed your complaining and prompted your gratitude.

God's Word:

I will praise you always
for what you have done.
I will proclaim before the faithful
that your name is good.

PSALM 52:11

Music

Beautiful music can lead us to God, echo the sentiments of our hearts, and bring us closer to one another.

A magnificent symphony, gifted soloist, or splendid choir can lift us to the Creator of all beauty.

The songs of slaves, those many ballads popular with lovers, and the victorious sounds of a marching band after its team scores a touchdown echo the sorrow, love, and joy often found in the human heart.

"God Bless America" became the uniting song of citizens across the country after the events of September 11, 2001; worshipers feel close when they join together in a famous and familiar version of the Lord's Prayer; a sing along of Christmas carols puts participants in an identical frame of mind for the holiday season.

Beautiful music can in fact lead us to God, echo the sentiments of the human heart, and bring us closer to one another.

Spiritual suggestion:

Remember a time when some beautiful music raised your spirit to God, or echoed the feelings in your heart, or bonded you to a group of people.

God's Word:

Sing to the LORD a new song;
sing to the LORD, all the earth.

PSALM 96:1

A Leader Who Prays

Dr. Condoleezza Rice is the first woman to ever hold the post of national security advisor to the President of the United States.

The daughter of a minister, she prays on her knees every night. She also offers little prayers all the time throughout the day.

Rice often prays simply that she will walk in God's way and not her own.

On the weekend after the 9/11 tragedy, she met with the President and his top advisors at Camp David. There must have been enormously high tension and great worry at that meeting.

To comfort herself and the others present, Rice sang a moving spiritual "His Eye is on the Sparrow and I Know He Watches Me."

Spiritual suggestion:

Have you ever gotten down on your knees and prayed? Try to imitate Dr. Rice by often praying throughout the day. Like her, make this your frequent prayer: "Lord show me your way and help me to walk in that path."

God's Word:

To you, I pray, O LORD;
at dawn you will hear my cry;
at dawn I will plead before you and wait.

PSALM 5:3–4

Eye Contact and a Smile

Sr. Anne Bryan Smollin is a nun who quietly listens to people as a professional therapist. However, as a popular lecturer around the country, she delivers rapid fire, high-energy talks about stress.

One of her suggestions for reducing stress is to make eye contact with people we meet and then smile at them.

Since hearing her speak, I have tried this out a few times walking down the street and at the busy local mall.

It works.

Instead of being preoccupied with my own concerns, I consciously sought to connect with the eyes of strangers, then smile at them. They often smile back.

I feel better and more relaxed. I bet they do, too.

Spiritual suggestion:

To reduce your own stress and the stress of others, try making eye contact with a few people and give them a smile.

God's Word:

When the LORD restored the fortunes of Zion,
then we thought we were dreaming.
Our mouths were filled with laughter;
our tongues sang for joy.
Then it was said among the nations,
'The LORD has done great things for them.'
The LORD had done great things for us;
Oh, how happy we were!

PSALM 126:1–3

Day 80

A Vision of Heaven

The cover of *Newsweek's* August 12, 2002, issue carried this title: "Visions of Heaven" and in the background reproduced artist Fra Angelico's famous painting of paradise.

A poll conducted by the magazine found that about 75 percent of Americans believe in heaven and think it is an actual place. However, opinions about the nature of heaven vary greatly.

My own Catholic tradition has this vision of paradise, heaven, or life after death.

We see God face to face.

We are reunited with deceased people who were close to us in this life.

We suffer no more pain or sorrow.

We still, in a mystical way, can connect with, love, and help people on earth.

This is a most comforting vision when we grieve over the loss of one we love or face death ourselves.

.

Spiritual suggestion:

Consider your own beliefs about heaven.

God's Word:

To you I raise my eyes,
to you enthroned in heaven.
Yes, like the eyes of a servant
on the hand of his master,
Like the eyes of a maid
on the hand of her mistress,
So our eyes are on the LORD our God,
till we are shown favor.

PSALM 123:1–2

Forgiveness

During the late '70s, I lectured for a month in South Africa, each week in a different city.

The ugly signs of apartheid were everywhere present: separation with preferential status for whites or so-called Europeans; separation with restrictions and oppression for blacks and colored or non-Europeans.

Nelson Mandela, a black leader, protested this injustice. To still his voice, the government imprisoned him for twenty-seven years.

When apartheid finally ended and a more just nation emerged in 1994, Nelson Mandela, released from jail, became the president of the new government.

Diplomats from around the world came for this memorable inauguration. But of all the guests attending perhaps the most intriguing were the three jailers or guards from that prison invited by Mandela himself.

That man with such a huge, forgiving heart is an inspiration to each one of us.

Spiritual suggestion:

Consider this example of Nelson Mandela and ask if it moves you to be as forgiving of others?

God's Word:

A clean heart create for me, God;
renew in me a steadfast spirit.
Do not drive me from your presence,
nor take from me your holy spirit.
Restore my joy in your salvation;
sustain in me a willing spirit.

PSALM 51:12–14

Gratitude

Last week, a couple at church asked me to pray for them. The husband had just been diagnosed with a supposedly malignant growth and, as always, the "C" word brought fear and worry into their hearts.

We prayed together for a few moments.

This week, the couple was back, and gave me some remarkable news. In the operating room and ready for surgery, the doctors discovered that the nasty lump had simply disappeared.

Was it a wrong diagnosis, a fluke of some kind, or a miracle? Could it have been an act of divine intervention?

Whatever the reason, the couple is overjoyed and most grateful to God for this response to their prayer.

Recognizing with gratitude every good thing as a gift from above frequently helps us feel the presence of God in our lives.

Spiritual suggestion:

Identify several good things that you experienced yesterday and give thanks to God for these instances of the divine presence in your life.

God's Word:

Say to God: 'How awesome your deeds!
Before your great strength your enemies cringe.
All on earth fall in worship before you;
they sing of you, sing of your name!

PSALM 66:3–4

Perseverance

My stepfather lost his mother under tragic circumstances when he was thirteen. He also grew up during the depression and tasted the bitterness of being poor.

However, through persistent hard work he became a successful businessman and was highly regarded in the road construction industry.

I clearly remember my stepfather—I called him Pop—saying to me when I was an adolescent that, "when everything seems to go wrong, when the clouds of our lives are very dark, if you keep plugging along, keep persevering, eventually something opens up and the sun begins to shine."

The Bible promises that those who persevere until the end will be saved. We might adapt this a bit and say that if we keep working, keep persevering in our efforts, we will surely survive, and even emerge victorious.

Spiritual suggestion:

Let this example and teaching about perseverance sink into your being so it will sustain you when future difficult challenges enter your life—as they will.

God's Word:

Forsake me not, O LORD;
my God, be not far from me!
Come quickly to help me,
my Lord and my salvation!

PSALM 38:22–23

Developing Our Gifts

Sir James Galway grew up in Belfast, Northern Ireland, where he mastered the pennywhistle as a young child. Later, at several single flute competitions, Galway won first prize and then decided to pursue music as his life's career.

That meant, however, years of hard work and study, beginning as a piano tuner. He subsequently studied musical theory and perfected his skills in London, Paris, and the United States.

That work and study produced great results. Galway has recorded more than fifty albums, performed throughout the world, and been honored by the Queen of England.

A sold-out audience gave Sir James and the Syracuse Symphony standing ovations not only at the end, but several times during the concert.

God blessed Galway with a great gift. But he has developed that talent through hard work—much to the delight of millions.

Spiritual suggestion:

Have you worked hard to use well and to develop fully a unique gift God has bestowed upon you?

God's Word:

How can I repay the LORD
for all the good done for me?
I will raise the cup of salvation
and call on the name of the LORD.
I will pay my vows to the LORD
in the presence of all his people.

PSALM 116:12–14

Focus in Our Lives

The Emergency Medical Services employees of Rural Metro in Syracuse and other similar ambulance agencies carry out very stress-filled tasks.

They receive an urgent call and, with lights flashing and siren screaming, rush to the location. There they must deal swiftly with an unconscious or seriously ill person who is often surrounded by deeply troubled family members. Quickly traveling to the nearest available hospital, they are forced to make and take life and death decisions and actions. At the hospital they entrust their patient to emergency room personnel.

Suddenly, the experience is over. After completing the necessary paperwork, they simply wait for another summons, seldom knowing what happened to this patient with whom they had been so intimately involved only moments earlier.

At a graduation ceremony for several of these emergency workers, the speaker reminded them of the enormous stress involved with their tasks. To deal with that tension, he cautioned the graduates to maintain a proper focus and to make adequate rest, exercise, and recreation a high priority.

Spiritual suggestion:

Keeping our focus and making sufficient rest, exercise, and recreation a priority are essential steps in coping with stress-filled work and lives.

God's Word:

I will bless you as long as I live;
I will lift up my hands, calling on your name.
My soul shall savor the rich banquet of praise,
with joyous lips my mouth shall honor you!
When I think of you upon my bed,
through the night watches I will recall
That you indeed are my help,
and in the shadow of your wings I shout for joy.
My soul clings fast to you;
your right hand upholds me.

PSALM 63:5–9

Praying Always

I recently heard this story about a taxi driver and a priest; both had died and were waiting for God's judgment upon them.

God asked about their occupations, and then gave the taxi driver a magnificent outfit and elegant mansion.

God gave the priest a shabby set of clothes and a run-down house.

The annoyed and puzzled priest asked God for an explanation. God replied: "When you preached, people slept; when he drove, people prayed."

It is good to pray when we are worried, but also good to pray when things are going our way.

Spiritual suggestion:

A Catholic blessing upon couples at their wedding reads this way: "May they both praise you when they are happy and turn to you in their sorrows." What good advice for all of us.

God's Word:

But I shall sing of your strength,
extol your love at dawn,
For you are my fortress,
my refuge in time of trouble.
My strength, your praise I will sing;
you, God, are my fortress, my loving God.

PSALM 59:17–18

Mistakes and Sins

We have a very conscientious and hard-working young man as a new employee. The other day, however, he seemed too worried about making a mistake and was feeling terribly guilty about it.

Many of us do the same, confusing perfectly human mistakes with morally wrong actions.

For example, we forget to set the alarm, drop a dish at dinner, or are in a clearly no fault accident.

That is different from carelessly being late, throwing a plate in anger, or injuring someone while driving under the influence.

For the one, we regret our human mistakes and accept our limitations.

For the other, we repent of our morally wrong actions and ask God to forgive us and heal our guilt.

Spiritual suggestion:

Cite an example from your past of a purely human mistake and a morally wrong action. Did you experience regret for the first and guilt for the second? Did you accept your limitations on one and did you ask God's forgiveness for the other?

God's Word:

How long, Lord? Will you utterly forget me?
How long will you hide your face from me?
How long must I carry sorrow in my soul,
grief in my heart day after day?

PSALM 13:2–3

Understanding

As a pastor in Fulton, New York, thirty years ago, I taught religion early in the morning to a cluster of eighth graders.

One day, I projected a slide with a dozen words on it like water, fire, and wind, asking the students these questions: Which word most represents God for you? Which one least represents God to you? Why?

That exercise held their attention for about five minutes, except for one girl who was doodling on a piece of paper at her desk.

Annoyed at this lack of interest and attention, I sharply asked her: "Mary, what about you?"

She quietly replied with embarrassment: "I forgot my glasses and can't see the figures."

There was no lack of respect there, no bad attitude.

When another's actions annoy or hurt us, we might first, with love, go beneath the surface and ask why.

Spiritual suggestion:

Understanding, the practice of going beneath the surface and asking why when the actions of another annoy or puzzle us, is a fundamental ingredient or aspect of love.

God's Word:

LORD, you have probed me, you know me:
you know when I sit and stand;
you understand my thoughts from afar.
My travels and my rest you mark;
with all my ways you are familiar.
Even before a word is on my tongue,
LORD, you know it all.
Behind and before you encircle me
and rest your hand upon me.
Such knowledge is beyond me,
far too lofty for me to reach.

PSALM 139:1–6

Dealing with Grief

Theodore Roosevelt had a great day and felt "full of life and happiness." As a member of the New York State Assembly, he had facilitated passage of several bills. Roosevelt had also just received a telegram from New York City indicating that his young wife Alice had given birth to their first child.

Things changed drastically several hours later. Another telegram arrived announcing that Alice was now dying of Bright's disease.

He rushed home and for several final hours held in his arms this woman he loved so much.

Following Alice's death, Roosevelt told himself that the only way he could survive was to dislodge her, to remove her from his soul. He tried to do that. Except for two brief written farewells, Roosevelt never mentioned Alice's name again.

That entire incident stunned me, both the sudden, totally unexpected tragedy and his unusual reaction afterwards.

Spiritual suggestion:

For most people, talking with others about their losses can help preserve warm memories and ease the pain of grief.

God's Word:

Lord, let know my end, the number of my days,
that I may learn how frail I am.
You have given my days a very short span;
my life is as nothing before you.
All mortals are but a breath.

PSALM 39:5–6

Giving

Dr. Marybeth McCall, now Chief Medical Officer at Syracuse's Crouse Hospital, began her career working in an emergency room practicing CPR. A homeless person in cardiac arrest was one of her first patients.

As she worked on the man, he would grab the lapels of her white coat, then let go. Later, regaining consciousness, he told Dr. McCall that he had seen God in heaven, but needed to come back to earth and ask forgiveness from his family for the hurts that his lifestyle had inflicted upon them. Later the man died quite peacefully.

Dr. McCall considers that this early giving of herself gave a homeless man the chance to give of himself and to heal relationships he had broken in the past.

Pope John Paul II maintains that only self-giving will fully satisfy the human heart.

Spiritual suggestion:

Think of a way you have given of yourself and the satisfaction you derived from that self-giving

God's Word:

Happy those whose way is blameless,
who walk by the teaching of the LORD.

PSALM 119:1

God as Our Leader

On a fall day driving on the New York State Thruway, I spotted a flock of birds heading south. They were in the familiar V formation with the leader heading toward a body of water for an overnight stay on their journey to a warmer home.

Is it not remarkable how God's creation naturally raised up this leader to guide these birds?

God, as our own leader, guides us in much the same way.

God encourages us to let go, overcome our reluctance, and leave a comfortable spot for a better place.

God stays in front of us, pointing out the right direction, and providing rest areas where we can catch our breath and regain our energy.

God finally brings us to a safe and serene home, far superior to one we just left.

Spiritual suggestion:

Trust in God as your leader, who encourages you to abandon a comfortable spot, guides you on life's journey, and takes you to a better place.

God's Word:

Be my rock of refuge,
a stronghold to save me.
You are my rock and my fortress;
for your name's sake lead and guide me.
Free me from the net they have set for me,
for you are my refuge.
Into your hands I commend my spirit;
you will redeem me, LORD, faithful God.

PSALM 31:3–6

Time for Solitude and Prayer

The Saint Columban Center in Derby, New York, just south of Buffalo, overlooks Lake Erie. This retreat house with extensive grounds touching the waterfront welcomes guests who come for a day, a weekend or a week of prayer. During that period, visitors listen to spiritual conferences and meditate, reflect and read religious books.

Banners attached to lampposts along the extended driveway greet visitors with this message: "Be still and know that I am God."

When retreatants depart, the reverse side of the banners sends them off with this blessing: "God be with you, wherever you go."

Those quiet hours of prayer and reflection away from busy lives help guests return home and resume work more conscious that God is always walking by their side.

Spiritual suggestion:

We need some time set aside each day for quiet prayer, if we are to be conscious that God is always walking by our side.

God's Word:

I will extol you, my God and king;
I will bless your name forever.
Every day I will bless you;
I will praise your name forever.
Great is the LORD and worthy of high praise;
God's grandeur is beyond understanding.

PSALM 145:1–3

DAY 93

Temptations

Our plane took off from Syracuse during a fairly heavy rainstorm. Within a short time we were passing through several of those fluffy clouds with their remarkable and beautiful configurations.

Most were pure white, although some had touches of darkness within them. The white ones were awesome, looked like huge balls of cotton, and seemed harmless enough.

The pilot, however, following radar guidance, gently swerved first one way and then the other to avoid them. Later and higher, we had the blue sky above us and a solid layer of such clouds beneath us.

When we descended to land, the turbulence within those apparently innocuous clouds reminded us that they were in fact quite dangerous.

In our own lives, sometimes certain objects, situations, and actions likewise seem attractive and enticing to us, but really can be harmful and should be avoided.

Spiritual suggestions:

Reflect upon past temptations and how they, by their very definition and nature, are attractive and enticing, but inner stirrings usually warn us that, beyond those glittering surfaces, trouble lurks.

God's Word:

God, you know my folly;
my faults are not hidden from you.

PSALM 69:6

Being Open to New Developments

When you are older in age and conservative in temperament, as I am, new experiences like these three can cause stress.

I flew Jet Blue for the first time knowing it was less expensive, but expecting only bare bones service. To my surprise, the flight attendants were exceptionally cordial, enthusiastic, and helpful.

Next, my seatmate on the two-hour flight was a well-educated American helping poor farmers in a Central Asian nation. Back in Florida with his family for a brief respite, he observed his daughter one day conducting a simultaneous three-way conversation on the Internet with a friend now in Korea and another friend back in that Central Asian country.

Finally, arranging for my airport shuttle, I was given a large circular beeper, which would vibrate and display red dots when the van arrived. It did just that.

Being open to those new experiences reduced my stress and helped me grow.

Spiritual suggestion:

When a new idea, worldview, or way of doing things enters into our lives, we often immediately experience a negative emotional and physical reaction. If we let go and open ourselves to the innovation, we find that the stress disappears and we can sense our inner growth.

God's Word:

For with you is the fountain of life,
and in your light we see light.

PSALM 36:10

Coping with Adversity

My presentation that had been received quite positively on six previous occasions recently encountered an apathetic, almost hostile audience.

The participants' early stoic response shook my confidence and caused me to lecture without energy, enthusiasm or eye contact. Even though, after a break, I recovered somewhat and did much better during the half-hour question and answer portion, I felt very low and deeply troubled by the unexpected bad experience.

During the three-hour flight after my talk, I pondered what went wrong and how I would do this differently in the future.

I also used the technique that a Trappist monk had taught me several years ago to counteract discouraged and disturbed feelings. I consciously turned my thoughts away from the negative events to other topics and to God.

That process helped lift me from the down mood I was in and restored my serenity.

Spiritual suggestion:

Consciously fostering positive thoughts can mitigate the negative feelings we may experience after a setback or some adversity.

God's Word:

One thing I ask of the LORD;
this I seek:
To dwell in the LORD's house
all the days of my life,
To gaze on the LORD's beauty,
to visit his temple.

PSALM 27:4

Waiting to Understand and Accept

George became quite depressed when he learned that he had a heart ailment. An active person who exercised frequently, ate only natural foods, and didn't drink alcohol or smoke cigarettes, George could not understand how this could happen to him.

It took him months before he learned to rejoice at seventy over the good health he still possessed and to be grateful for the wellness he had previously enjoyed during his long life.

The parents of twenty-two-year-old Michelle suffered greatly watching their daughter deteriorate as a result of a serious blood disorder. They desperately sought out every available cure.

However, when the inevitable death drew near and her sufferings intensified, their attitude changed. Now they were willing, even anxious, to let her go so she would be free of all pain.

Spiritual suggestion:

Like seventy-year-old George and like Michelle's parents, we frequently must go through periods of waiting, sometimes lengthy ones, before we can understand and accept a major burden in our lives.

God's Word:

Wait eagerly for the LORD,
and keep to the way;
God will raise you to possess the land. . . .

PSALM 37:34

Keeping the Sabbath

In Genesis, the first book of the Bible, we read that, after having created the heavens and the earth, God rested on the seventh day and blessed it. (Genesis 2:1–2). Later God said, "Keep holy the Sabbath day. Six days you may labor and do all your work, but the seventh day is the Sabbath of the Lord, your God." (Genesis 20:9–10).

Christian, Jewish, and Muslim people take that command seriously, gathering for public prayer or worship and spending the day in rest or recreation.

Muslims do so on Friday.

Jewish people observe the Sabbath from sundown Friday to sundown Saturday.

Most Christians make Sunday their seventh day to keep holy.

Setting aside one day each week for public worship and personal recreation sustains our connection with God, reflects our faith to others, and maintains a healthy balance in our lives.

Spiritual suggestion:

Examine the way you observe the Sabbath.

God's Word:

O God, you are my God—
for you I long!
For you my body yearns;
for you my soul thirsts,
Like a land parched, lifeless,
and without water.
So I look to you in the sanctuary
to see your power and glory.
For your love is better than life;
my lips offer you worship!

PSALM 63:2–4

A Noble Deed

For many years, Ron Lanz has been driving a truck on a regular route between the Midwest and the East. He expects to retire soon, but an unusual incident may change those plans.

En route east, listening to the radio, Lanz heard descriptions of a blue Chevrolet Caprice allegedly used by the sniper who had shot a dozen people and caused great fear among residents around the nation's capital.

A short time later, he pulled over, according to his custom, at a familiar suburban Maryland rest area to use the bathroom facilities.

Returning to his tractor-trailer, he spotted a car that seemed to match the description given, dialed 911, and informed police of his observation and location.

Later, the truck driver told media people that he was no hero, only doing what seemed right. Moreover, Lanz said that if he received any of the promised $500,000 reward, at least some of it would go to the families of people killed by the snipers.

Spiritual suggestion:

Consider the empowering example of the noble deeds of others, and how you can imitate them.

God's Word:

Merciful and gracious is the LORD,
slow to anger, abounding in kindness.

PSALM 103:8

Wounded Human Nature and Divine Healing Grace

Traveling by train from Syracuse to Toronto meant inspections at the border by United States and Canadian customs officials. After one uniformed agent checked my documents, another walked rapidly down the aisle shouting, "A dog is coming."

A dog indeed was coming, loosely held in check by the officer as it swiftly sniffed all corners of the car. The trained canine was obviously seeking dangerous drugs, explosives, or firearms. What an unfortunate waste of time, money, and resources.

I reacted to that experience as I do when passing through airport detectors, signing in before a guard at an office building, or looking at chained fences which surround so many buildings.

These security measures, while necessary, have only a negative function—to prevent people with evil in their hearts from hurting others.

They also are regular reminders of our own wounded human nature in need of God's healing power.

Spiritual suggestion:

Think of how that familiar spiritual "Amazing Grace" captures the dual reality of human existence: the presence of sin and evil coupled with the need for divine forgiveness and healing.

God's Word:

LORD my God, in you I take refuge;
rescue me; save me from all who pursue me. . . .
PSALM 7:2

Laughter

In his first published book, a priest author tells this story:

A man from Chicago left the snow there for a sunny vacation in the south. His wife, on a business trip, expected to join him the next day.

After settling in at a Florida hotel, he decided to send his spouse a brief e-mail message. However, the husband had misplaced her e-mail address. Nevertheless, relying on his memory, he typed in the information.

Unfortunately, the man had one character wrong, and sent his communication instead to the elderly widow of a preacher who had died the day before.

When the grief-stricken woman checked her e-mail, she screamed, then fainted. Her family members rushed into the room and discovered these words on the monitor:

"Dearest wife. Got checked in. Everything prepared for your arrival tomorrow. P.S. Sure is hot."

Spiritual suggestion:

If you laughed as hard as I did when I read this story, then reflect on how humor and the laughter that accompanies it do reduce stress.

God's Word:

May God be gracious to us and bless us;
may God's face shine upon us.
So shall your rule be known upon the earth,
your saving power among all the nations.
May the peoples praise you, God;
may all the peoples praise you!

PSALM 67:2–4

Dealing with Adversity

Having malfunctioning knees and hips, being a hemophiliac or a bleeder, and suffering a half dozen major surgeries would test anyone's spirit. Moreover, this man, who now walks well, but slowly, with the help of a walking stick, once thought his entire life would be spent in a wheelchair.

How did and does he cope with such adversity?

The memory of his mother's courage helps him. He remembers well how this single mother bravely struggled with life's challenges.

The human spirit's remarkable strength likewise sustains this man. He was surprised during the darkest moments by how his inner self had enough resources to bear these burdens and bounce back so swiftly.

Finally, faith in God, who is close to the brokenhearted and near to those crushed in spirit, was the ultimate source of this man's ability to weather these storms and emerge with the serene smile he displays today.

Spiritual suggestion:

We can find strength from several sources to help us deal with adversity: the heroic example of others, the amazing strength of the human spirit, and faith in God.

God's Word:

In you, LORD, I take refuge;
let me never be put to shame. . . .
Do not cast me aside in my old age;
as my strength fails, do not forsake me. . . .
God, you have taught me from my youth;
to this day I proclaim your wondrous deeds.
Now that I am old and gray,
do not forsake me, God,
That I may proclaim your might
to all generations yet to come,
Your power and justice, God,
to the highest heaven.

PSALM 71:1, 9, 17–19

Afterword

Now, with the 101 days completed, if you have not experienced some reduction in stress and an increase of stillness within your soul, write to me and I will send you a check refunding the price of this book.

Father Joseph Champlin
Cathedral of the Immaculate Conception
259 East Onondaga Street
Syracuse, New York 13202

Resources

These spiritual suggestions have emerged from my own lived experiences, "urban legends," a few presentations by others, and my own reading.

These volumes served as the source for ideas or stories on the days indicated:

Day 12	Tom Brokaw *The Greatest Generation*
13	Lawrence Jenco *Bound to Forgive*
23	Lance Armstrong *It's Not About the Bike*
24	Patrick Carnes *Out of the Shadows*
30 & 35	Ron Wooten Green *When the Dying Speak*
34	Robert Barron *The Strangest Way*
39	David K. O'Rourke *A Process Called Conversion*
42	William Bennett *The Moral Compass*
49	Nicholas Sparks *A Bend in the Road*
53, 62, 66	Edmund Morris *Theodore Rex*

55 William Bausch *A World of Stories (For Preachers and Teachers)*

68 & 81 Colin Powell *My American Journey*

79 Ann Bryan Smollin *God Knows You're Stressed*

89 Edmund Morris *The Rise of Theodore Roosevelt*

100 Joseph Sica *Well, It's about Time!*

If I have neglected to credit properly other resources, I would be happy to make that correction in a future edition. Here, however, I wish to mention Fathers James Hayes and Shaun Mahoney whose words prompted the messages on Days 55 and 86.

As the introduction describes, this book gradually evolved over a two-year period and with the assistance of many people. I wish to express my deep gratitude to:

—Paul Cowley of Cowley Associates who made the initial suggestion about a spiritual message on the radio.

—Mary Dougherty, Account Executive for Clear Channels Communications in Syracuse, who arranged the time, financial details, and recording schedule.

—The marketing and production personnel at Clear Channels Communications who were so supportive at the very beginning and contributed many ideas at our initial focus session.

—Nia Carter who developed and recorded the tag line.

—Joshua Farrell, a production assistant at 570 WSYR, who has recorded all 101 of these messages.

—Stewart Hancock, publisher of Eagle Newspapers, who liked the radio spots and incorporated them into his weekly papers.

—Frank Cunningham and Robert Hamma at Ave Maria Press, who saw the possibilities of a book in these spiritual suggestions.

—Maureen Quirk as well as Ann, Julie, and Megan Tyndall, who typed the original radio messages on word processor, prepared the Index of Topics, and checked the written text for accuracy.

—Art and Pat Gale, who converted the handwritten and edited pages to a final printed text on disk ready for submission to the publisher.

—All those known and unknown people who on many occasions praised the radio spots and made so worthwhile the effort to offer these spiritual suggestions for a stress-filled society.

Index of Topics

Number(s) following each entry indicates day(s) the topic occurs.

Father Joseph M. Champlin is the rector of the Cathedral of the Immaculate Conception in Syracuse, New York. He has written more than forty books, including *Through Death to Life* and the bestselling *Together for Life.*

More Reflections for Busy Lives

GOD KNOWS YOU'RE STRESSED
Simple Ways to Restore Your Balance
ANNE BRYAN SMOLLIN

You *can* manage your stress. And this book will show you how, with thoughtful insights, practical suggestions, and the shared stories of others.

ISBN: 1-893732-35-5 / 160 pages / $11.95

DAYBREAKERS
365 Eye-Opening Reflections
CLIFFORD WILLIAMS

No time to think about the things that really matter? Take just a moment each day with these concise, significant reflections.

ISBN: 1-893732-52-5 / 128 pages / $10.95

CUP OF GRACE . . .TO GO
What Jesus Might Say to Start Your Day
ANITA M. CONSTANCE

Get your day off to a great start with a brief thought about your own hopes and concerns and reflect upon what Jesus might have to say in response today.

ISBN: 0-87793-965-9 / 112 pages / $8.95